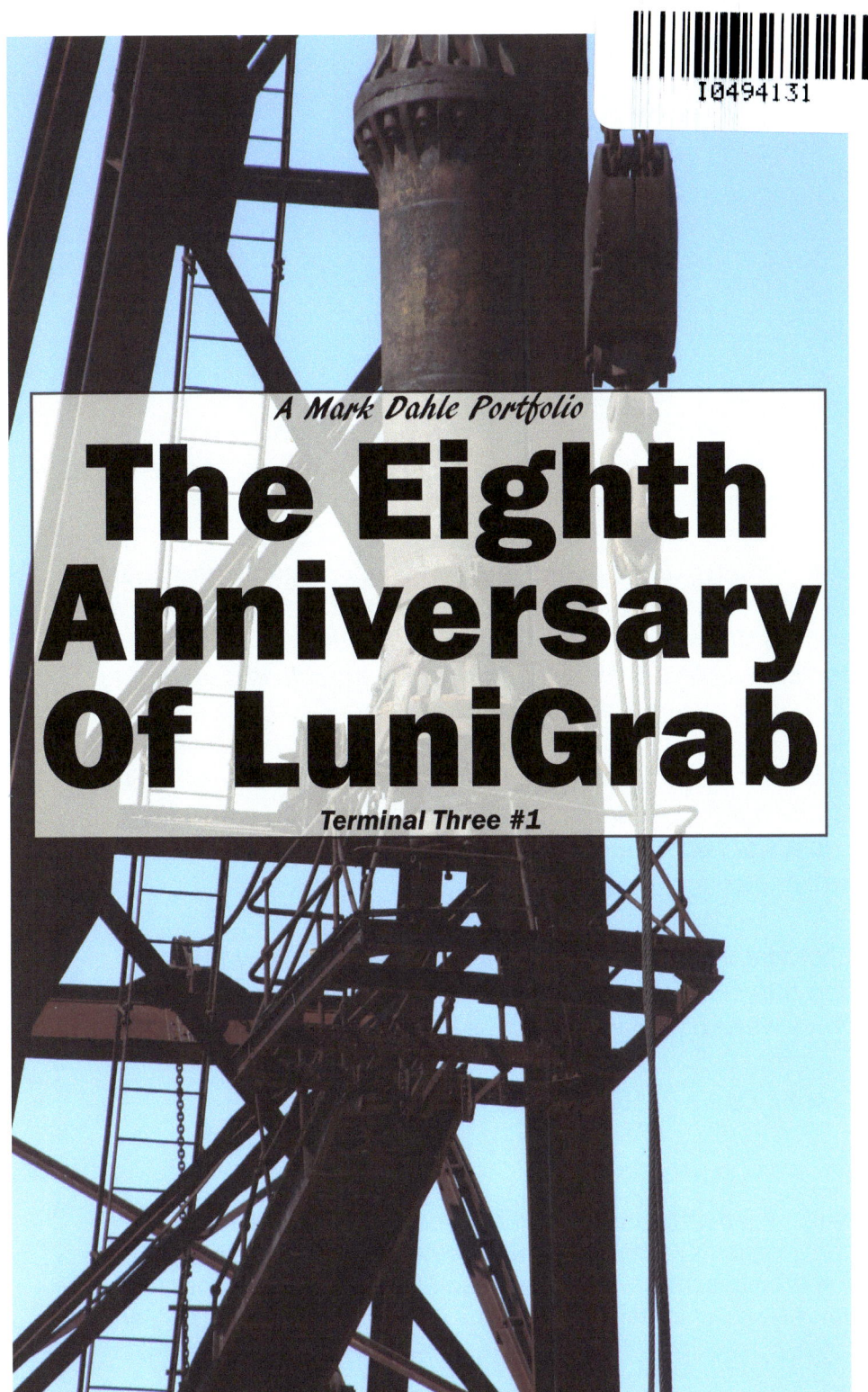

A Mark Dahle Portfolio

The Eighth Anniversary Of LuniGrab

Terminal Three #1

Mark Dahle Portfolios can be read in a few minutes and enjoyed for a lifetime.

Unlike many picture books, the text is not related to the beautiful painting at the right and the photographs that follow. This might seem a little weird at first. One thing that helps is to order more portfolios until you get used to it. In the meantime, feel free to draw your own pictures of Terminal Three if you like.

This portfolio includes a photo of a brilliant 36 x 24 inch painting (at the right), twenty-five beautiful pictures of Venice, Italy, and a story about member of the resistance on a mission to Whitehorse.

Photographs in this book are available in very limited editions. See http://www.MarkDahle.com for more information and for previews of upcoming portfolios.

We do our best to create portfolios free of editing mistakes. But it's hard to catch everything. We reward people who report errors in any Mark Dahle portfolio. For details see MarkDahle.com/Typos.html or email MarkDahle@aol.com with the subject line "Typos." Thanks!

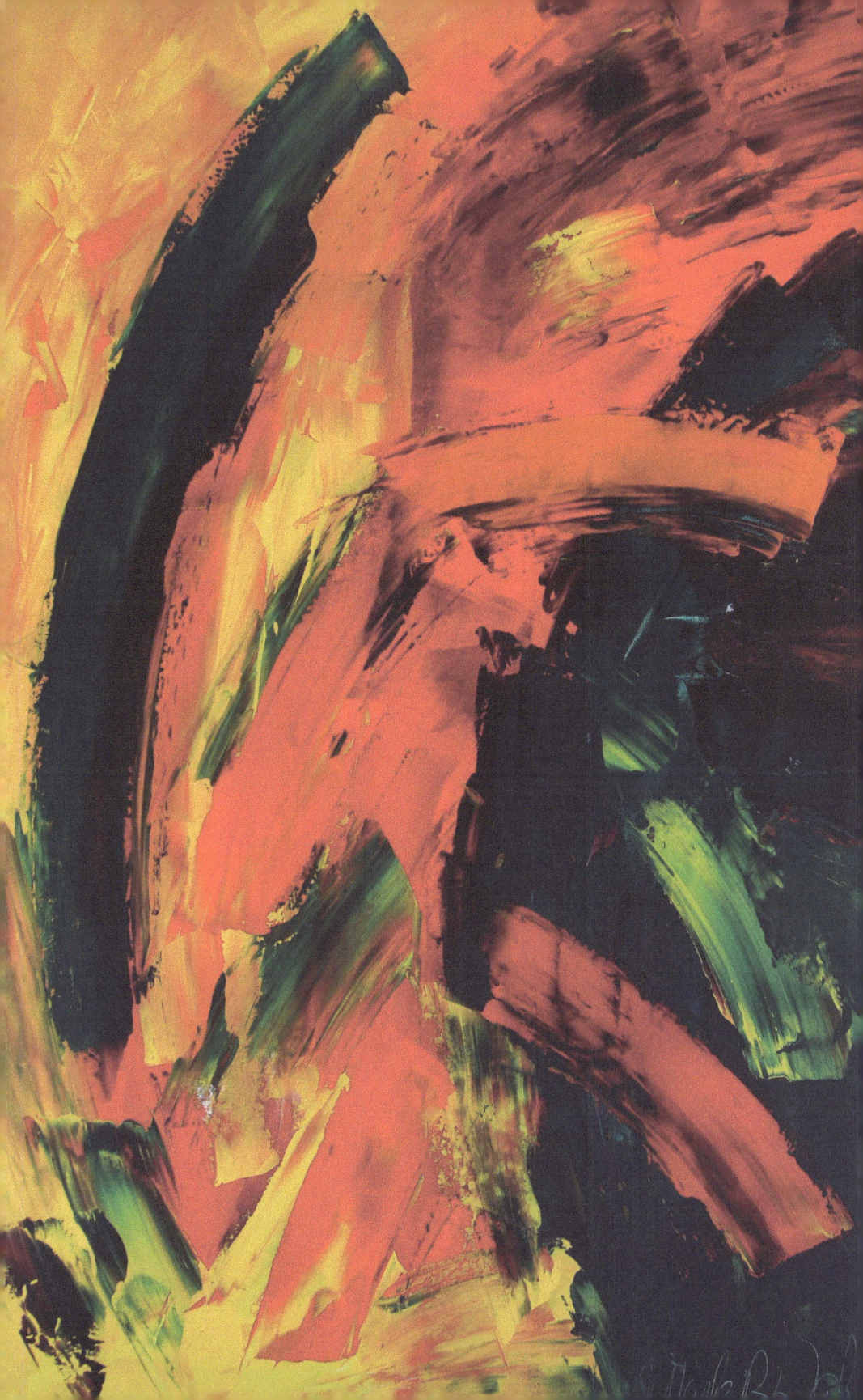

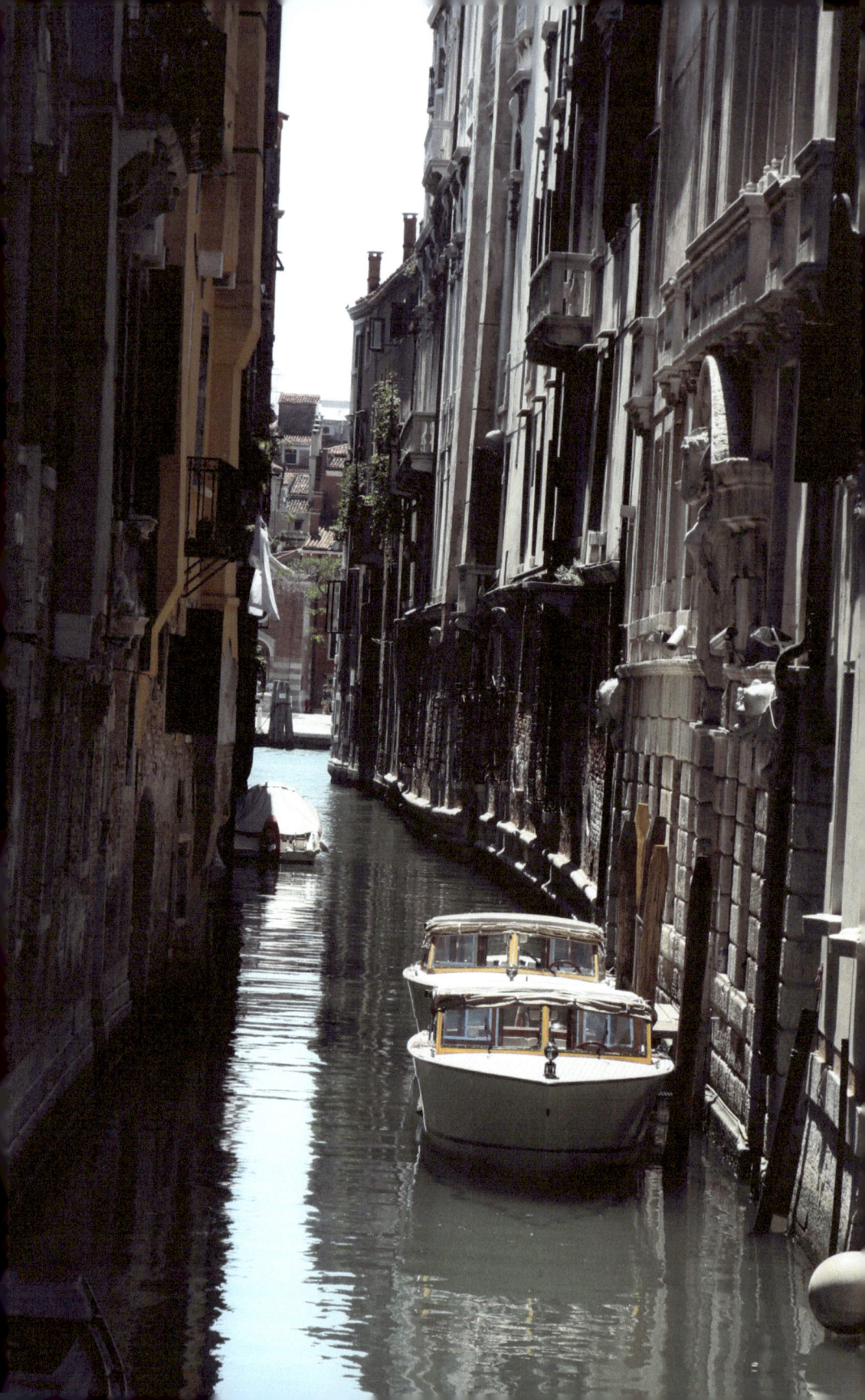

Normally Han would have ignored most of the airport announcements. But on the eighth anniversary of LuniGrab, right before the Otto Convention? No. *Everyone* expected trouble today. To be arriving at the crowded airport on such an anniversary felt like madness.

Han was walking down the long corridor to the entrance of Terminal Three when he heard the first announcement. By chance it was about the moon quadrants. That unsettled Han even more. If it was a sign, it was sure to be a bad one.

> *All visitors to Moon Quadrants A and C are advised that the MalPox quarantine is still in effect. Visitors will not be able to leave until the quarantine is lifted. The MalPox quarantine is expected to last up to two years. At present Quadrant A is 54 percent full, and food reserves are at 72 percent capacity. Consult your TravRep for a complete list of available supplies required and conditions before proceeding.*

> *The flight to Quadrant A is delayed for five hours because of solar static, but Quadrant C will be departing in ten minutes. This flight is nonrefundable due to the quarantine.*

> *For your safety, do not take Vivitol during transport.*

Han's only consolation about being at the airport on LuniGrab was that he was going to Whitehorse. Even in the summer nobody wanted to go near the radiation mines except workers. In winter his flight should be nearly empty. If there *was* trouble today, it would be somewhere strategic. Whitehorse was the safest location he could think of.

> *The flight to Lima is delayed two minutes because of ElectroHaze.*

> *Passengers waitlisted for Mexico City have been cleared. Departing in 3 - 2 - 1.*

When Han passed the IdoScan at the entrance to Terminal Three, an alarm sounded. He stopped, confused. Why would *he* set off an IdoScan? But it turned green and let him pass two seconds later, with no explanation.

Han tried to appear calm and shake it off. Looking jittery wouldn't help him stay alive today.

> *An explosion at Tokyo has closed the Kyoto sector for the next five hours. You may reroute through Pyongyang if you have Sector Nine clearance. People with tourist visas will need to reroute through Tokyo 4 or Tokyo 6 or reschedule for tomorrow.*
>
> *A reminder to all passengers: When your flight is announced, do NOT move or you will miss the port and you will need to be rescheduled. Missing two ports will result in a fine of 100 EuroZ.*

Han focused on maintaining his breathing and heart rate so they seemed normal. But he *was* jittery. He desperately wanted to see if Robert had left a message explaining his assignment.

All Han knew was that he was going to Whitehorse, a mining area that would be desolate and cold this time of year. Too cold. And he had to fly on the anniversary of LuniGrab, when everyone expected trouble. And he was part of a group he had never seen; he was to meet five people on the way. He had no other instructions.

> *Now boarding Los Angeles at Phoenix in 3 - 2 - 1. Los Angeles West departs in five minutes.*
>
> *Lima departing in 3 - 2 - 1.*
>
> *Now boarding all local flights under 500 miles. Ready in 3 - 2 - 1.*

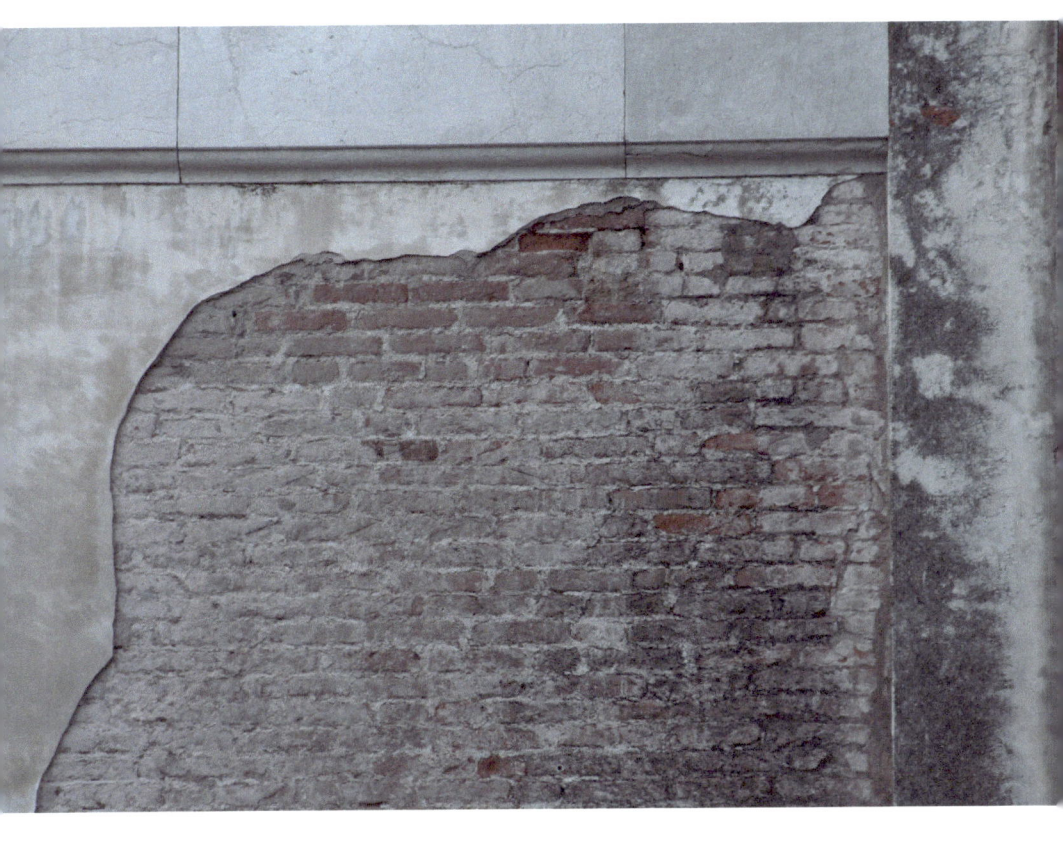

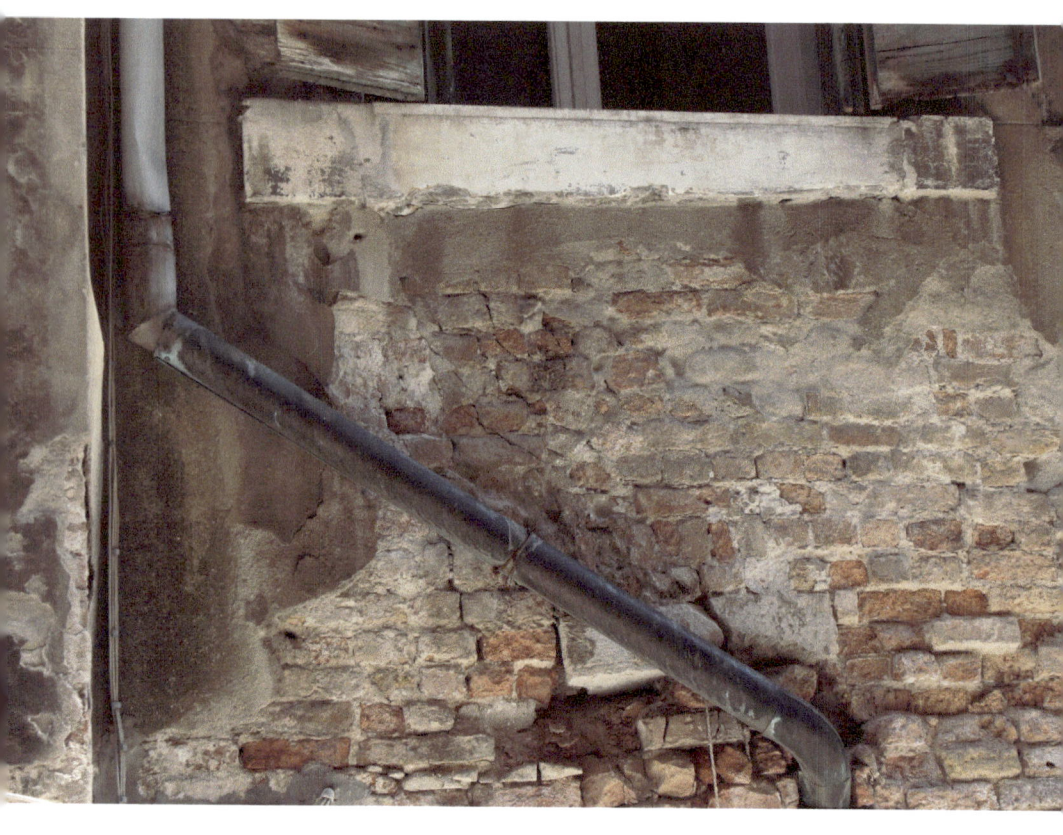

A chime sounded.

Attention Terminal Three.

The announcements preceded by a chime were security announcements. Often one had only seconds to comply or risk being ported to Confinement. Occasionally people not complying were simply executed. All the passengers around Han stopped what they were doing to listen.

> *Syniptograph readings indicate Threat Level 47. Passengers in Terminal Three must stop all activity immediately for a full sweep, to commence in ten seconds. Anyone remaining in motion will be immediately transferred to Gulag 48. The sweep begins in 3 - 2 - 1.*

The light shifted slightly, and Han waited. Out of the corner of his eye he could see a man move his arm. Was he drawing a weapon? Scratching his leg? The man instantly disappeared.

That man would regret that one move for a long, long time, Han thought. Gulag 48 was rarely used except for the worst cases of Espotage. To go straight there on a sweep meant the authorities were as nervous as the citizens. Everyone expected something today.

> *Translations of all messages are available on ports 222, 221, and 220. Engala cominico 2 2 2. Boograda cominico 2 2 1. F'rsook cominico 2 2 0. Estranza optima. Tout.*

> *Arrivals from Venus Six are now cleared with level Green. If you wish to achieve Black Zone status, please hold.*

The lights in the terminal returned to normal, indicating the end of the sweep.

The ConsoloGraph sometimes took a minute to analyze the data, but this time it was done in just a few seconds.

Terminal Three now clear.

Han instinctively checked his NewsGraph implant to see the results.

Four people were arrested in Terminal Three this morning for possession of dangerous materials. All threats in the terminal have been resolved.

Han continued to wait, motionless, watching others around him resume their regular activities. He saw two more people disappear before he started to move again.

It was the third time Han had seen that happen in a week. Han couldn't understand it. After the official count on the NewsGraph was released, more people disappeared. So far, all Han could think of was to stand motionless a few seconds longer than normal after each sweep.

> *Water rations are in effect in Jerusalem/Dubai. Do not travel to the region without adequate water for your entire trip.*
>
> *Amensica detonica denaspola. Partook. Defanisko et panglako.*

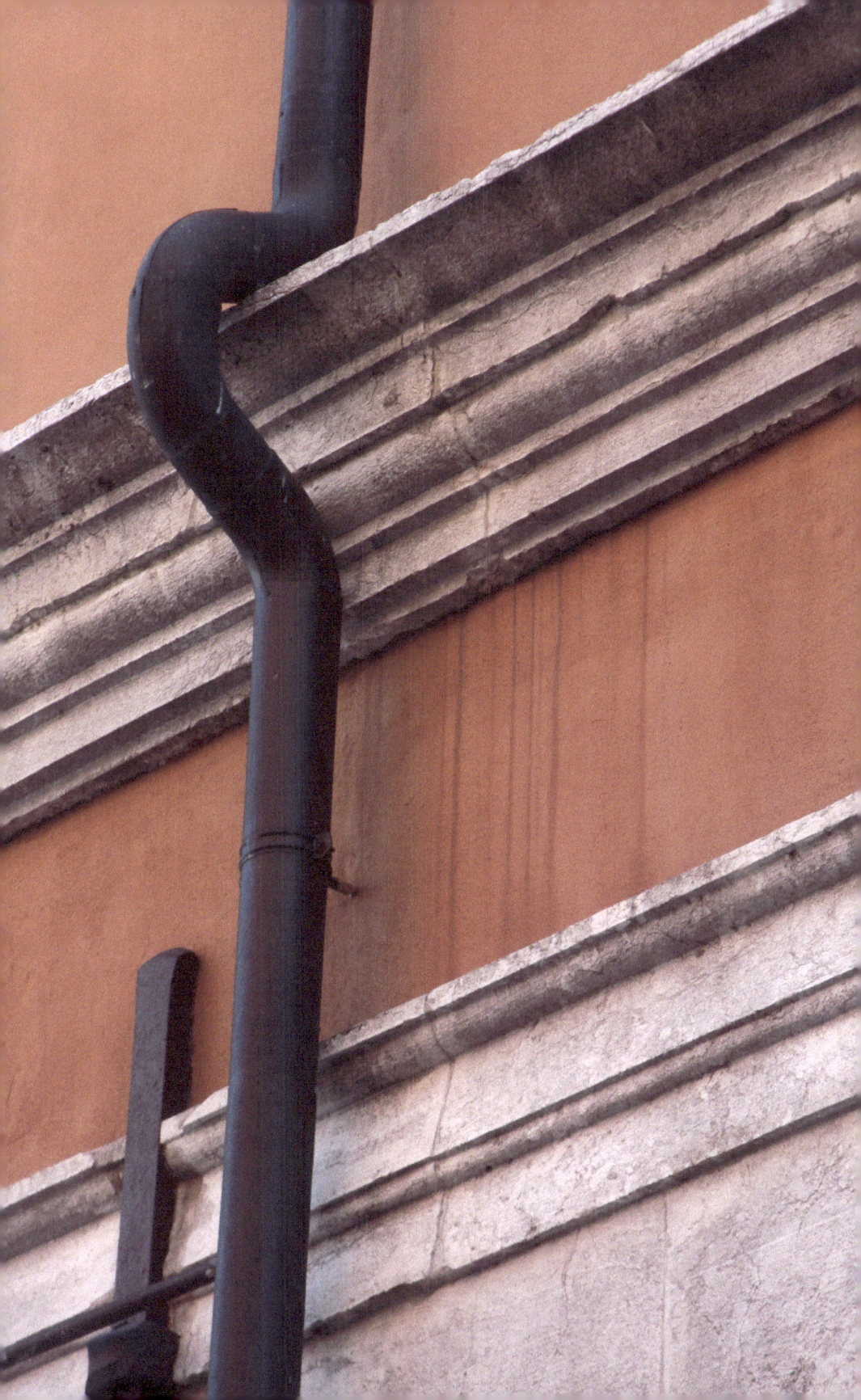

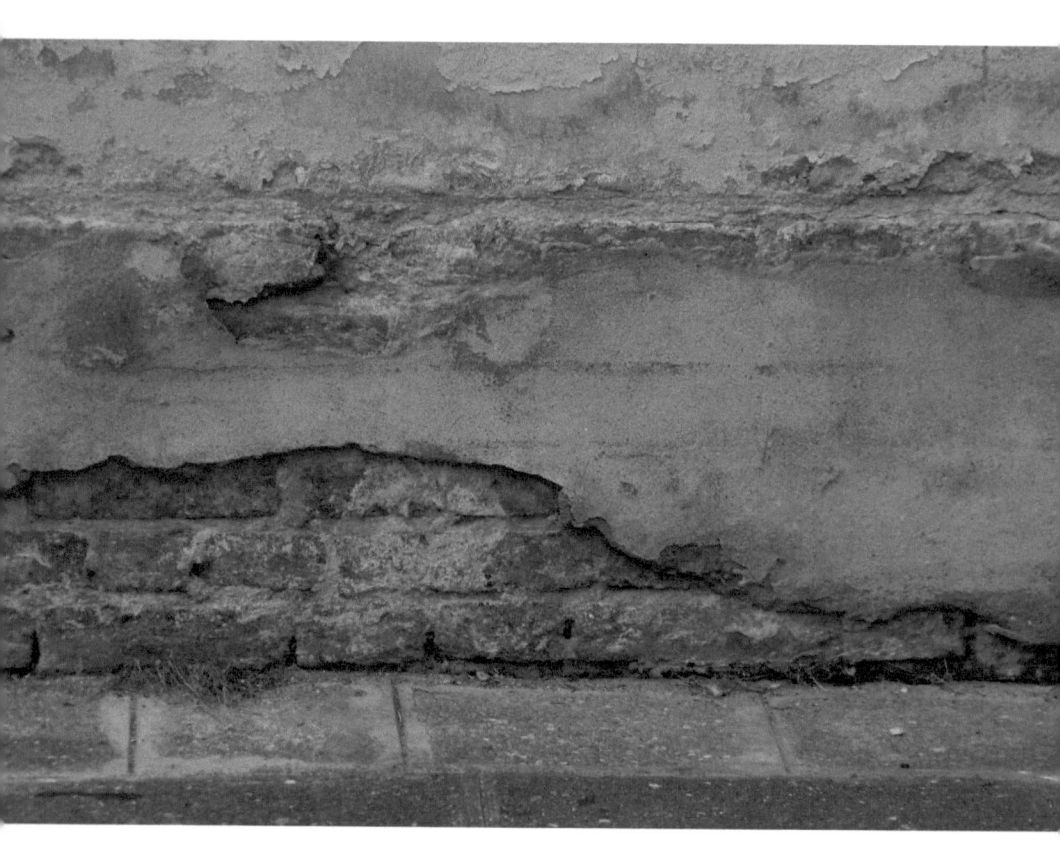

Han checked his AltiLevel. It was out of the normal range, but not yet life-threatening. He hoped he could avoid more sweeps. But given his present location, he knew the odds were low.

It is against the law to fly on behalf of anyone else, or to fly if you have not paid the full fare out of your own personal CheckAccount. If you are flying at the request of someone else or if someone else paid your fare, you must register immediately with ProtectaShield. Violators face fines of 150 EuroZ and possible conviction.

The last flight to Santori Ten has been canceled. Friz ended ten minutes ago, earlier than expected. We apologize to all passengers in the terminal. Your families on Santori will be notified. Transfers to Santori Ten will not be available until March or April, depending on conditions. Consult your NewsGraph for more details. Video transmissions are still possible for the next ten minutes. Do NOT purchase transportation from PediCab drivers to Santori Ten. People traveling outside sector 72 airspace will be prosecuted.

When Han had signed up with the resistance, he thought he might be sent on a mission to someplace like Santori Ten. Someplace far away. Someplace where it would be hard for him to get back. So he was surprised when he learned his instructions were as benign as going to Whitehorse. If he hadn't been told to travel on LuniGrab, he wouldn't have thought much about his assignment at all. Whitehorse would be cold, but at least the terrain and the predators would be familiar.

A reminder that Sao Tome has installed new protocols for all passports from the Southern Zone. Do not travel without consulting your NewsGraph. The delayed flight to Sao Tome will be ready in 30 seconds.

Because of high traffic to Chicago Minnesota, several flights have been re-routed to accommodate demand. Singapore, New Delhi, and the local to South Sudan are experiencing 15-minute delays. Four flights to Chicago Minnesota are standing by for departure. The first is departing in 3 - 2 - 1. The second flight to Chicago Minnesota has checked in full. Departing in 3 - 2 - 1.

Now departing for Sao Tome in 3 - 2 - 1.

Flight three for Chicago Minnesota: 3- 2 - 2 and holding – Citizen 45J9H stop moving, you are delaying the flight. Resuming 3 - 2 - 1.

Flight four missed its window because of the delay for flight three. Please listen for your flight to be called in the next few minutes.

Four scheduled flights to one location within a minute! That was something that hadn't hit the NewsGraph. And delaying New Delhi to accommodate traffic to Chicago Minnesota? Han's *mission* might look routine, but the day didn't.

Remember that TerFlax is prohibited on all flights. Traveling with TerFlax is a crime punishable by four years in Maximum for the first offense, and execution for the second offence.

West Palestine In Exile now available for boarding in 3 - 2 - 1.

East Palestine In Exile available only through locals at Shanghai. Now boarding Shanghai for immediate departure.

New Moscow now available in 3 - 2 – sorry – holding for equipment change – holding – 3 - 2 - 1.

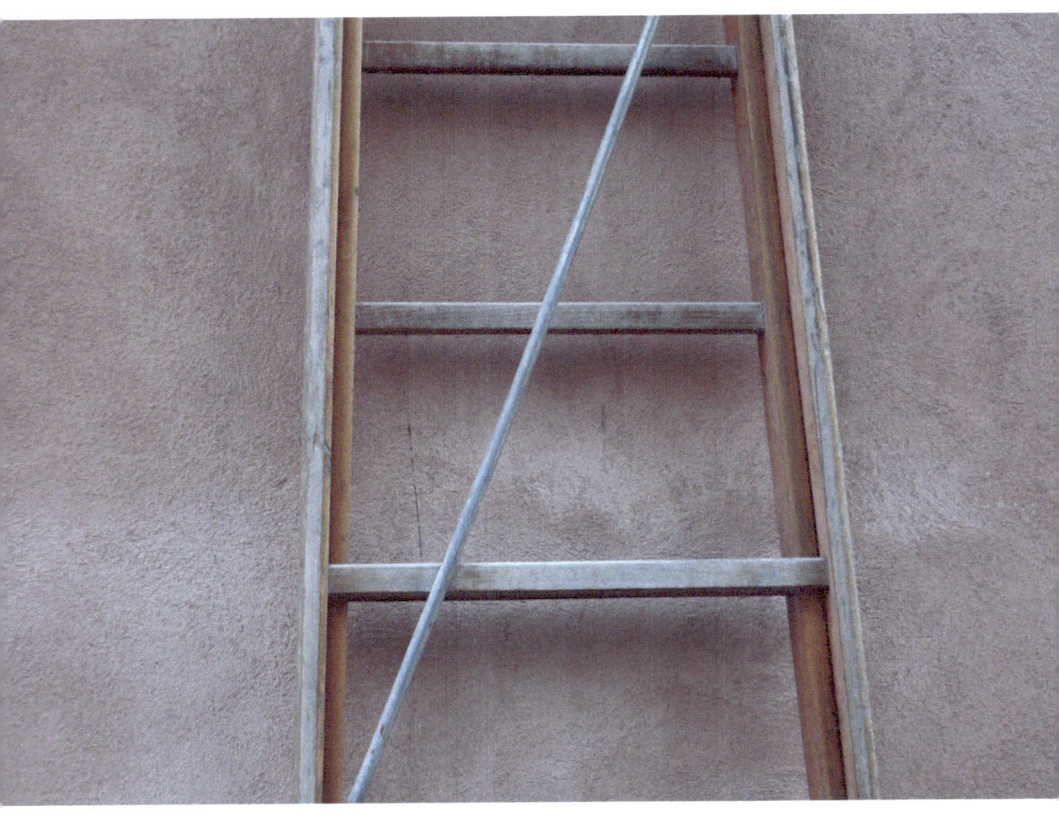

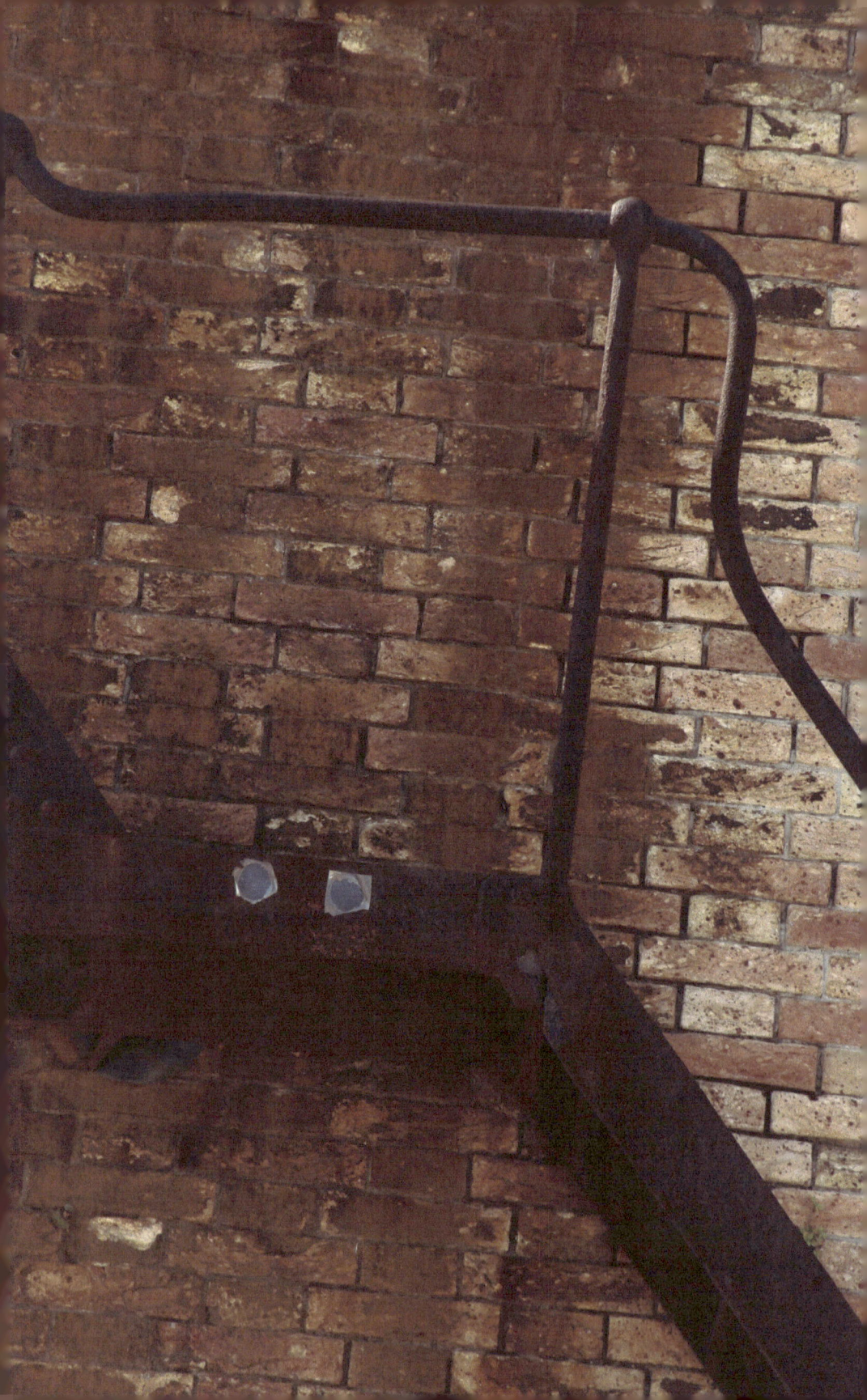

When Han had signed up to help the resistance, he said he would help no matter what the cost.

When he heard he was traveling on LuniGrab, Han wondered how high the cost might be. But everything seemed fairly routine so far. And his flight would be called soon.

> *Central Command welcomes all officers to Terminal Three. Status 5 and above please report to The CC Club in the Green Tower.*

> *Chicago Minnesota now boarding Simuflight Ten. Opt out if you wish to continue holding for a direct flight.*

The Simuflight was rarely used. It was one of the first prototypes of the new airport. Its advantage was that it could handle ten times more traffic than a normal airport. It parceled out the departure and arrival times, so it was slightly less predictable, but passengers didn't mind because they were exposed to BetaZone on the flight. These days it was one of the few ways to get BetaZone.

> *Simuflight Ten boarding complete.*

If the Simuflight was in operation today (and if it filled so quickly after three flights to Chicago Minnesota had already departed), the city itself must be nearing its travel capacity.

The next announcement confirmed Han's guess.

> *Passengers to Chicago Minnesota are advised that new protocols will be in place within ten minutes. You may travel on the next flight, due to depart in 60 seconds, or take any local from the Plains or Rocky West. Please signal your intentions within thirty seconds. Passengers not accommodated will be put on the standby list for Whitehorse.*

Han paused, surprised by the news. Whitehorse was a *long* way from Chicago. He tried to keep his heart rate from rising rapidly – he didn't want to trigger another sweep – while he checked his NewsGraph to see how people might route from the Whitehorse mines to Chicago.

The NewsGraph reported exactly what he had thought: It was not possible.

Then a new channel blinked open. For the next fifteen minutes, the Mine Corporation's Tube to Duluth was being opened for public transport. From Duluth you could catch a local.

Han realized with a start that such a route might be even better than the Chicago express, at least if you were going to the Otto Convention. The local could stop at the convention site far outside Chicago, eliminating all the traffic congestion around the airport.

Han guessed the main terminal at Chicago would be closed within an hour, maybe for several days, because of the traffic volume. Once people arrived, they'd likely stay through the end of the Otto Convention and no more travel visas to the area would be honored until someone left.

> *The last flight to Chicago Minnesota departs in 3 - 2 - 1.*

> *All remaining passengers are assigned to Rocky West, departing in 3 - 2 - 1.*

> *The next Rocky West local departure estimated at five minutes.*

> *All connections to Whitehorse have now checked in full. Tube upgrades are complete.*

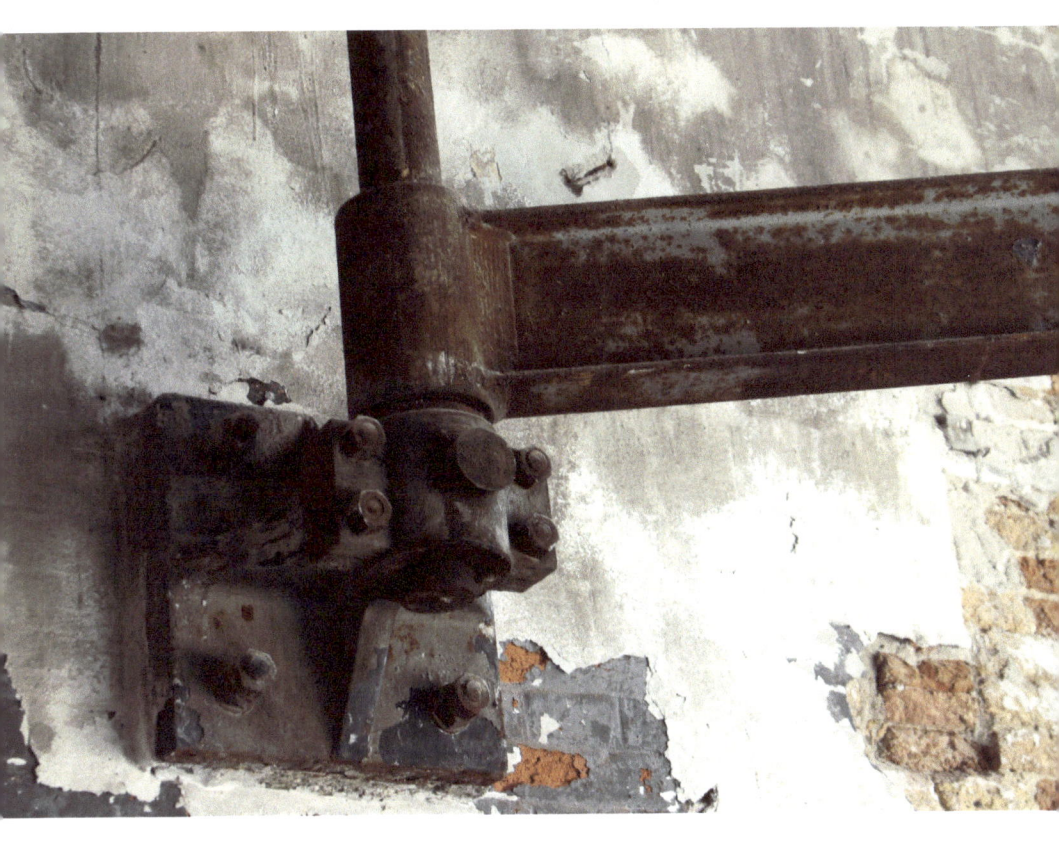

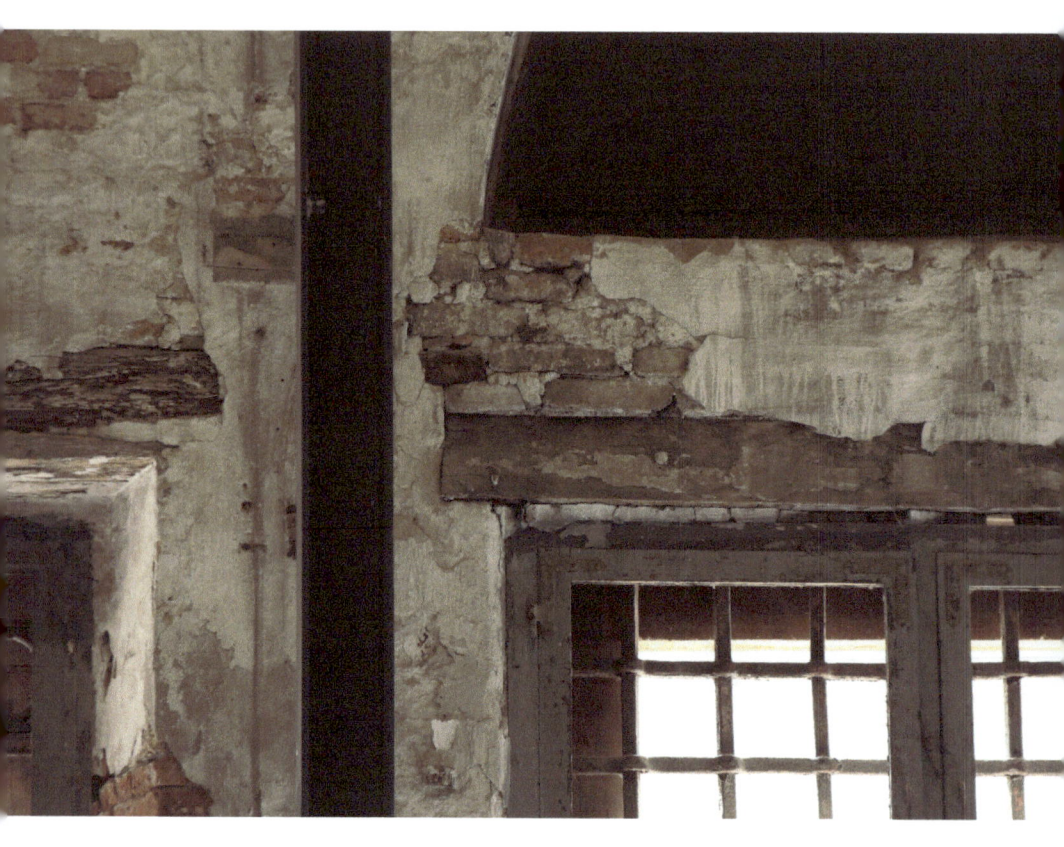

The announcement that Han's flight had suddenly completely filled made Whitehorse sound a bit more strategic and a lot less safe.

Han decided it was time to call Robert.

Although Robert's VerBox was well hidden, Han knew as soon as he called that Central Command would discover it and destroy it. If he called too early, his haste would destroy Robert's last chance to get him a message. But with the Whitehorse flight now full, Han wanted to call before the flight boarded and he lost the chance.

Han pressed the numbers for the VerBox and paused for the IDScan. The message began sooner than he expected.

"Hey! Just wanted to let you know I'm sending you a new Braazoid. Hope you like it. Over and out."

> *Because of heavy traffic, New York/Washington requires Pink Clearance today. If you do not have Pink Clearance, you must take the Baltimore local. New York/Washington departs in 3 - 2 - 1.*

> *Baltimore local will depart after all passengers who lacked Pink Clearance have been Securitized. Please stand by. Thank you. Process complete. Baltimore local departs in 3 - 2 - 1.*

"Over and out," Robert had said. That was the first code phrase Robert had ever mentioned to Han. It meant Robert expected to be dead by the time Han retrieved the message. It was the one code phrase Han had never expected to hear.

And a Braazoid? What would Han do with a children's game?

Saturn sectors 4 and C are now boarding for immediate on-time departure in 5 - 4 - 3 - 2 - 1. Saturn Sector 4 clear.

Saturn Sector C holding for less warpshift turbulence. We apologize for the delay. Saturn Sector C now ready in 3 - 2 - 1. Saturn Sector C clear. The next scheduled flight to Saturn is for Sector F in 59 hours.

Han checked his NewsGraph for deliveries. The Braazoid was there.

New Braazoids came out once a month, and Han had been sent the latest edition. This one was a game about lemmings. Han had just authorized its start when his NewsGraph went blank and rebooted. Han had been too slow. Central Command had noticed the VerBox communication and erased it and all associated files.

Vehicle 29YT will be impounded if not moved.

Because of the war violence in Berkistan, all InstaDot travel to that country was suspended today at 6 a.m. Conventional planes are still flying, with a 48 percent chance of landing. We do not advice travel to Berkistan at this time.

Han ported to the gift shop in the terminal to see if they had Braazoids. He didn't know if Robert had sent him something off the shelf or if he'd gotten a modified version with something hidden in it. If he'd been sent a special version, it was already erased. Han's only hope was that Robert's message was part of the game itself, something available on all the releases.

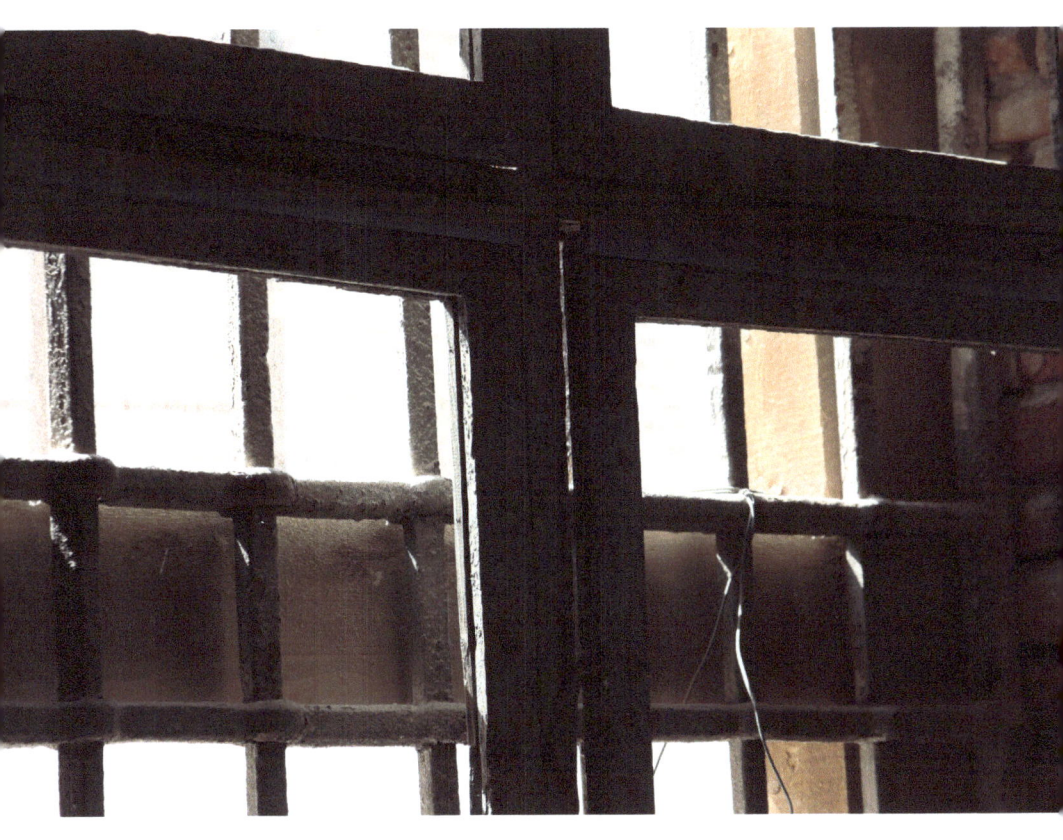

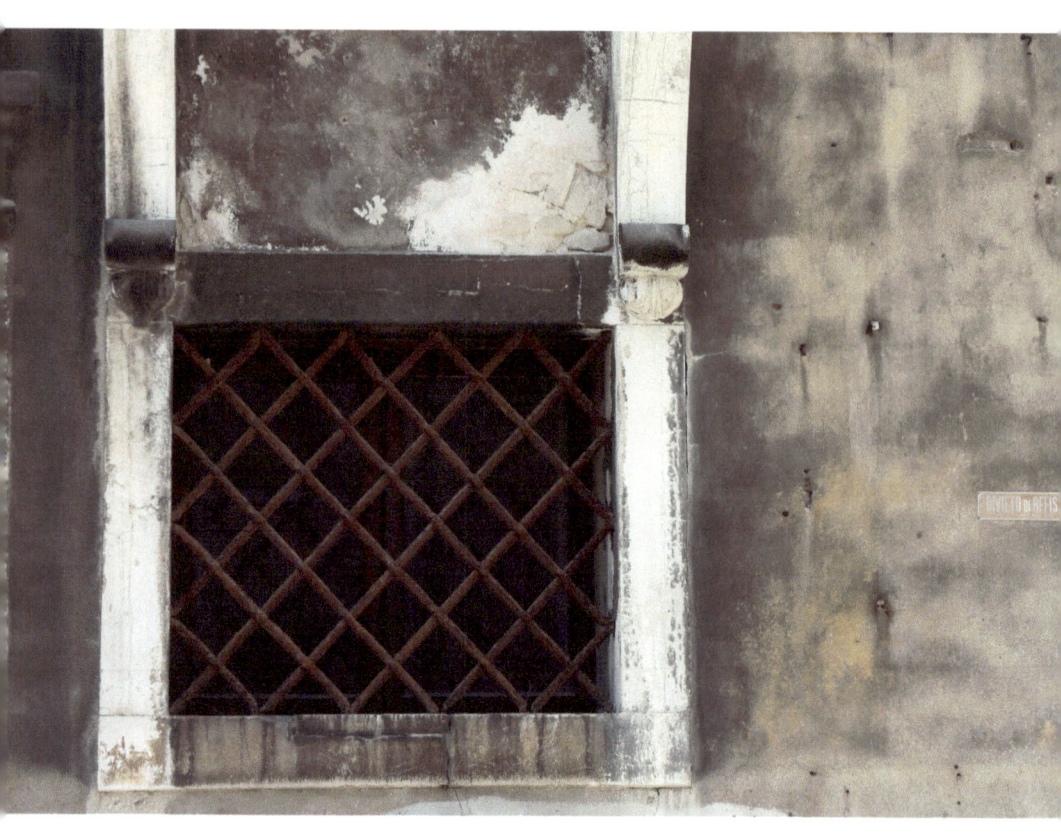

Attention Inbound from Venus Six: all Black Zone applications have been processed. Please check your monitor to determine the status of your request.

Bjergisnord kondicontacal 8 8 y.

The last flight to Venus Two departs in two hours. Venus Two will be out of range for the rest of the year. LifePro options must be secure before leaving on this flight.

The gift shop's Braazoid display had dozens of copies of the latest edition. Han didn't dare download the game so soon after it had been deleted on his NewsGraph; Central Command would surely notice. Instead, he watched the demo version in the store display.

In the demo, lemmings were jumping off a cliff. The object of the game was to stop them. The tagline for the game came up at the end of the demo: "Don't be first." Then the promotion looped and started again.

Now departing for Rome, Paris/Madrid, and Beijing in 3 - 2 - 1.

A reminder to all passengers traveling on local flights: the maximum baggage allowed is 38 hectas. If you are traveling with more, you must declare Customs.

Local service now available for the Plains, Rocky South, and Texico. All points depart in 3 - 2 - 1.

Han's NewsGraph pinged, indicating that his flight was about to be called. He had no more time to watch the demo. Han hoped the message he was supposed to get was simple. "Don't be a lemming." Or maybe "Stop the lemmings." Or "Don't be first." One of those. If it was anything more complicated, Han was out of time to discover it.

His NewsGraph pinged one more time, and he heard the airport announce his flight.

Whitehorse departs in 3 - 2 - 1.

The first part of any journey at the airport was short. When flight departures were announced, passengers were ported to a secure waiting room that would become their transport vehicle after the HealthScan. Some rooms held dozens of passengers; at least one could hold ten thousand. Han was surprised to find he had been ported to the largest room at the airport. And it was full.

Once the passengers were ported to the room, a HealthScan was run. It was usually complete in 60 seconds. Then they would be off. The transport to a place as close as Whitehorse might take 15 seconds. Even Santori Ten took less than a minute.

Announcements in the waiting area were restricted to those that applied directly to their transport. For the first time since he arrived, Han relaxed slightly. No more need to filter the incessant messages. From now on, any messages would apply to their flight. They would be departing soon.

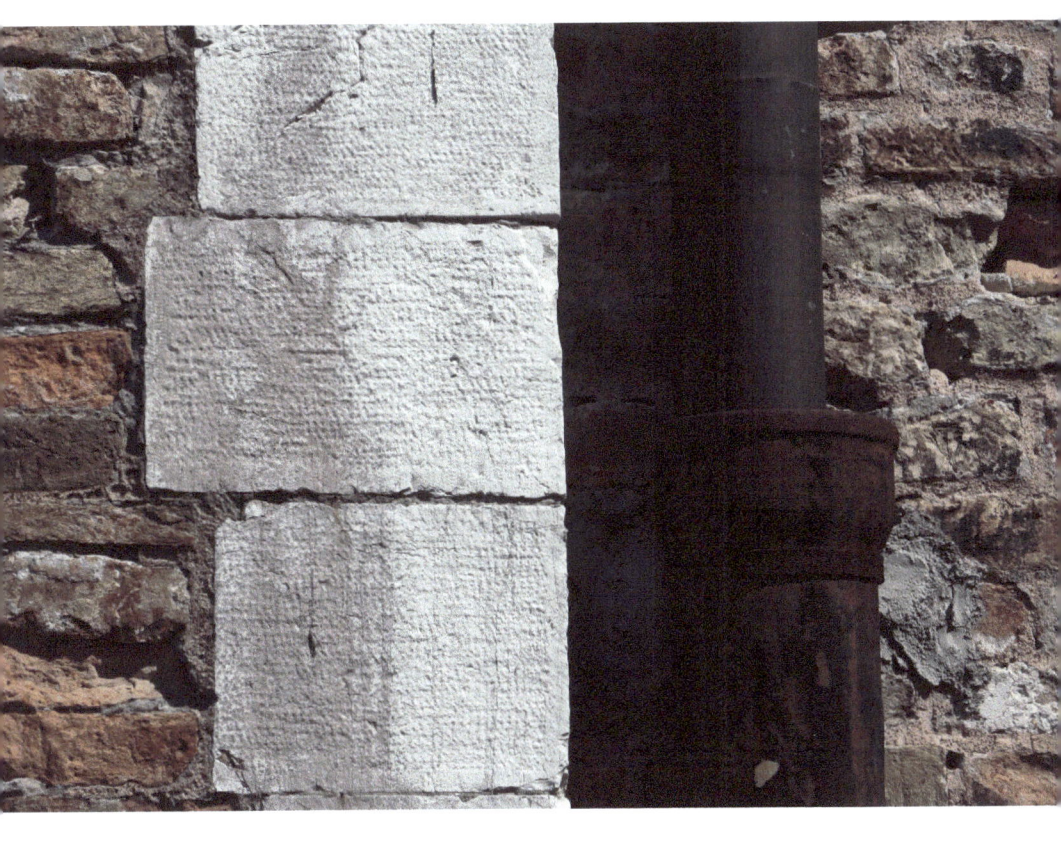

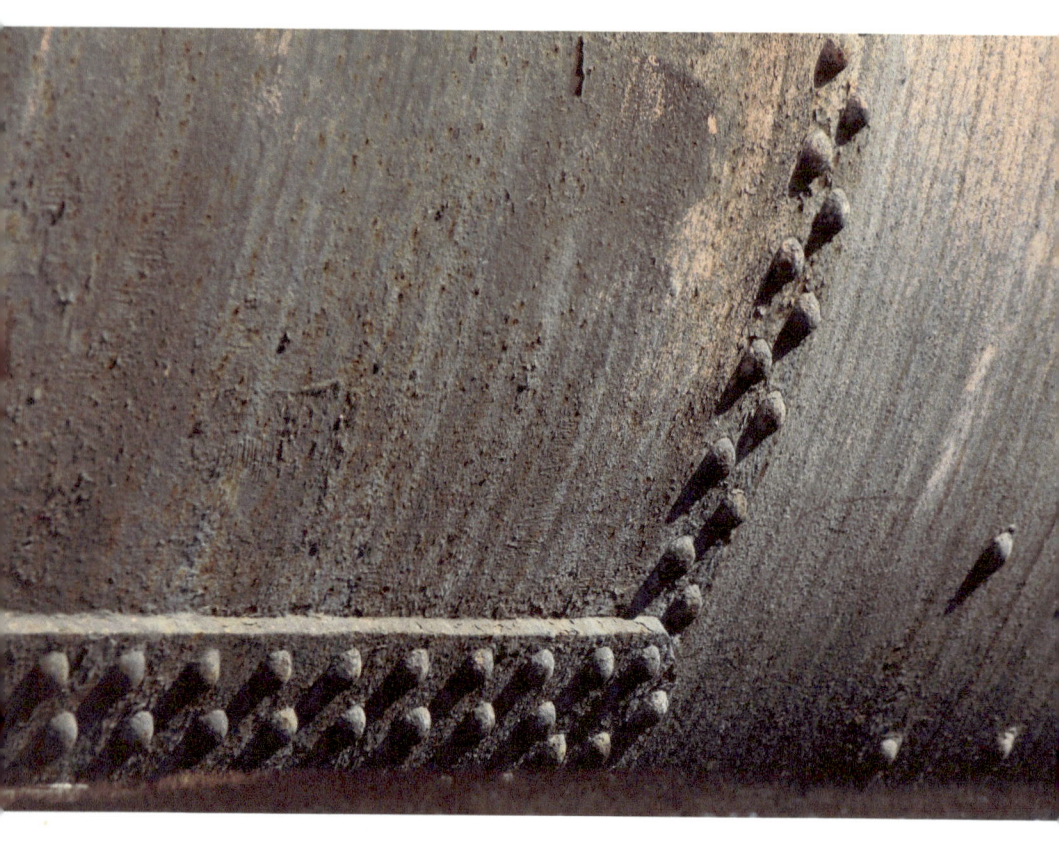

If Robert's message was "Don't be first" and it applied to Han's arrival at the waiting area, he had been successful. The waiting room, normally spacious and empty, was completely jammed. Han had never seen a flight so full.

But if the instructions were "Don't be a lemming," Han thought he probably was less lucky.

> *Due to congestion at Whitehorse airport, your flight is experiencing a brief delay. Please stand by. Your HealthScan will commence when your flight is ready.*

Hearing the announcement, Han suddenly realized that *other* airports were also scheduling flights to Whitehorse. Whitehorse was not going to be deserted when he arrived.

It took five minutes before congestion at Whitehorse cleared somewhat and their flight was placed back in the queue.

> *The HealthScan for your flight will begin in three seconds.*

> *Thank you. The scan is now complete.*

Han estimated about ten passengers had disappeared during the scan, at least of those he could see.

When he had signed up with the resistance, the only question they pursued with vigor was whether he was completely healthy. Now he saw why. Any sign of disease and he would have been bumped from the flight. Perhaps even the mission itself would have been aborted.

> *We apologize for the delay due to congestion at Whitehorse. Your flight will depart shortly.*

As soon as the HealthScan was over, Han could tell something inside him had changed. He had a brief flash of an image: a worm with a white head inside his brain, sniffing, looking for release. Han frowned. Where had *that* idea come from? He was completely healthy; he had just passed a Health Scan.

But then he saw a motion, out of the corner of his eye. A passenger close by on his left touched his throat. The passenger had been smiling before the scan, then afterwards he touched his throat. It wasn't much, and without Han's own discomfort, he was sure he wouldn't have noticed. But he'd seen videos from Quadrant C, and it was a familiar gesture. All the government volunteers on the Moon's Quadrant C that got MalPox died within 60 seconds of their first symptoms. Many had briefly touched their throats.

Han shook himself. The moon's Quadrants A and C were quarantined. And the whole flight to Whitehorse had been cleared by the HealthScan. But as he watched, he saw a woman on his right shake her head also, a worried expression on her face, a bead of perspiration forming on her upper lip. As the countdown for launch began, he saw a passenger straight ahead wobble slightly.

> *Attention Whitehorse passengers. Your flight will depart in twenty seconds. Do not move between the time that transport begins and your arrival is announced. Transport begins in 15 - 14 - 13 - .*

Han glanced at the passengers near him. He could count six, including himself, who showed signs of discomfort. Six passengers in his immediate area who had been cleared by the HealthScan moments before now appeared ill at ease. If they were all feeling as bad as he suddenly was, it was unprecedented. He couldn't imagine the odds of such an event. And how did they manage to be so close together in a room that held thousands of passengers?

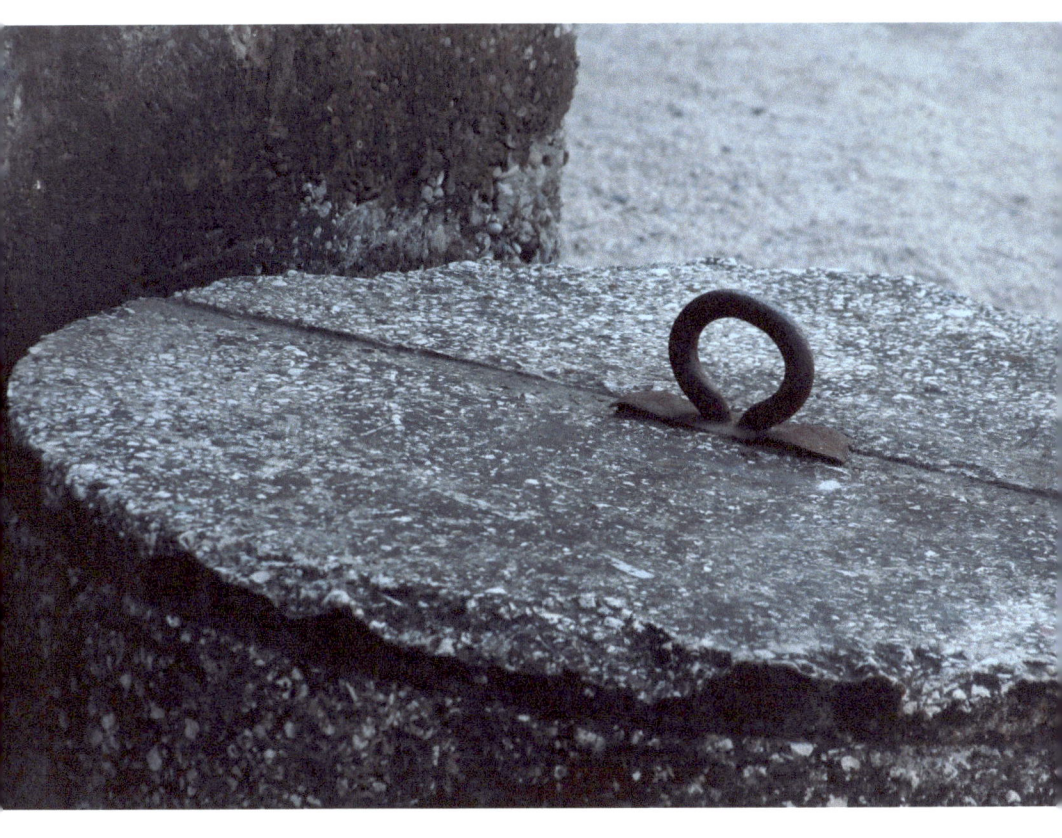

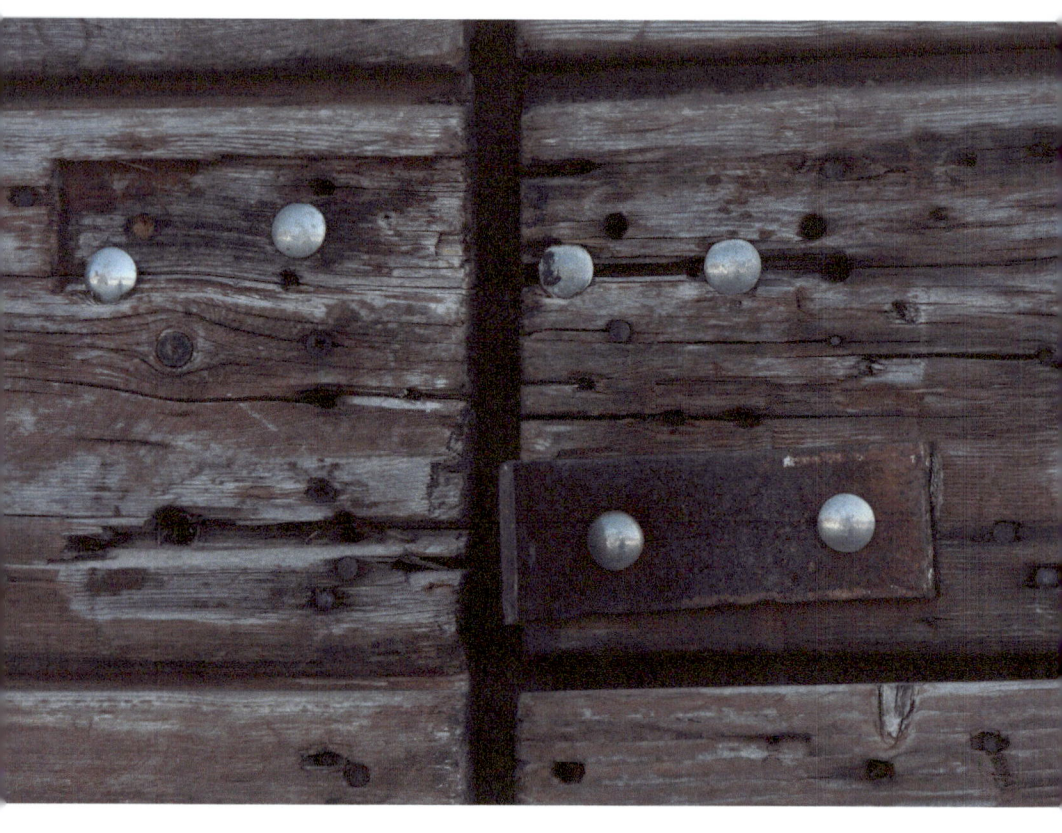

Han straightened his body to be ready for the transfer, but his knees felt like buckling. When his ComJac buzzed, he checked it without thinking. It was Robert, telling him he needed to be by an exit door.

Han's head was swimming. He made his way toward the exit without thinking, vaguely aware that the other five he had picked out were headed the same direction. Han tried to focus; he had to get to the exit before the countdown ended and motion was forbidden.

When he arrived at the exit doors, he realized he was positioned to be first out once the flight arrived at Whitehorse. His fever was spiking and it was difficult to think, but the "Don't be first" tagline crashed into his consciousness at the same time he remembered Robert's "Over and out." The latter phrase meant Robert had expected to die before Han could retrieve the Braazoid. He hadn't sent the code for all clear in the message to get close to an exit. Was Robert really still alive and sending messages? If not, who had told Han to move?

3 - 2 - 1 -

The transfer began. Han was sweating freely, both from the fever and what he was thinking. By mid-transport he was sure that someone had faked Robert's last transmission, someone who hadn't known what Robert's "Over and out" code had meant.

What had Han's original assignment been? He could barely focus. "You'll know your assignment when you meet the five others on your team to Whitehorse."

If Han had guessed right about the team, they were all sick, maybe with MalPox. And if that was what they had, they would be dead in half a minute. The rest of the passengers would be dead a few minutes after that. Almost everyone in Whitehorse would be dead by the weekend.

Infecting Whitehorse mine workers wasn't what Han had imagined when he had signed up to help the resistance. But it didn't seem to matter now.

Han was nauseous.

The video screen above the exit door showed the approaching terminal area. He could see a vast swirling crowd.

Han coughed. Once. Then he forced himself to stop. He could not appear sick; the mission would fail if he drew too much attention to himself. But by now he had all the symptoms. His vision was blurring and MalPox was exploding inside his system.

Han braced for impact.

Arrival was announced, the doors opened and his consciousness returned, briefly, in time to register the crowds. Han's swirling vision presented images that looked more like a hallucination than reality. Red hats, yellow hats, streamers, yellow and red buttons. It looked like a party.

An Otto party, some part of his brain reported.

Han was going to step toward the crowd but his last bit of consciousness stopped him for the briefest instant. "Don't be first," it said.

Luckily for Han, one short pause was enough. A woman on his right, one of the five he had identified, lurched past him, convulsing more than walking. As she stumbled past an IdoScan, the alarm went off and she was instantly surrounded by security guards.

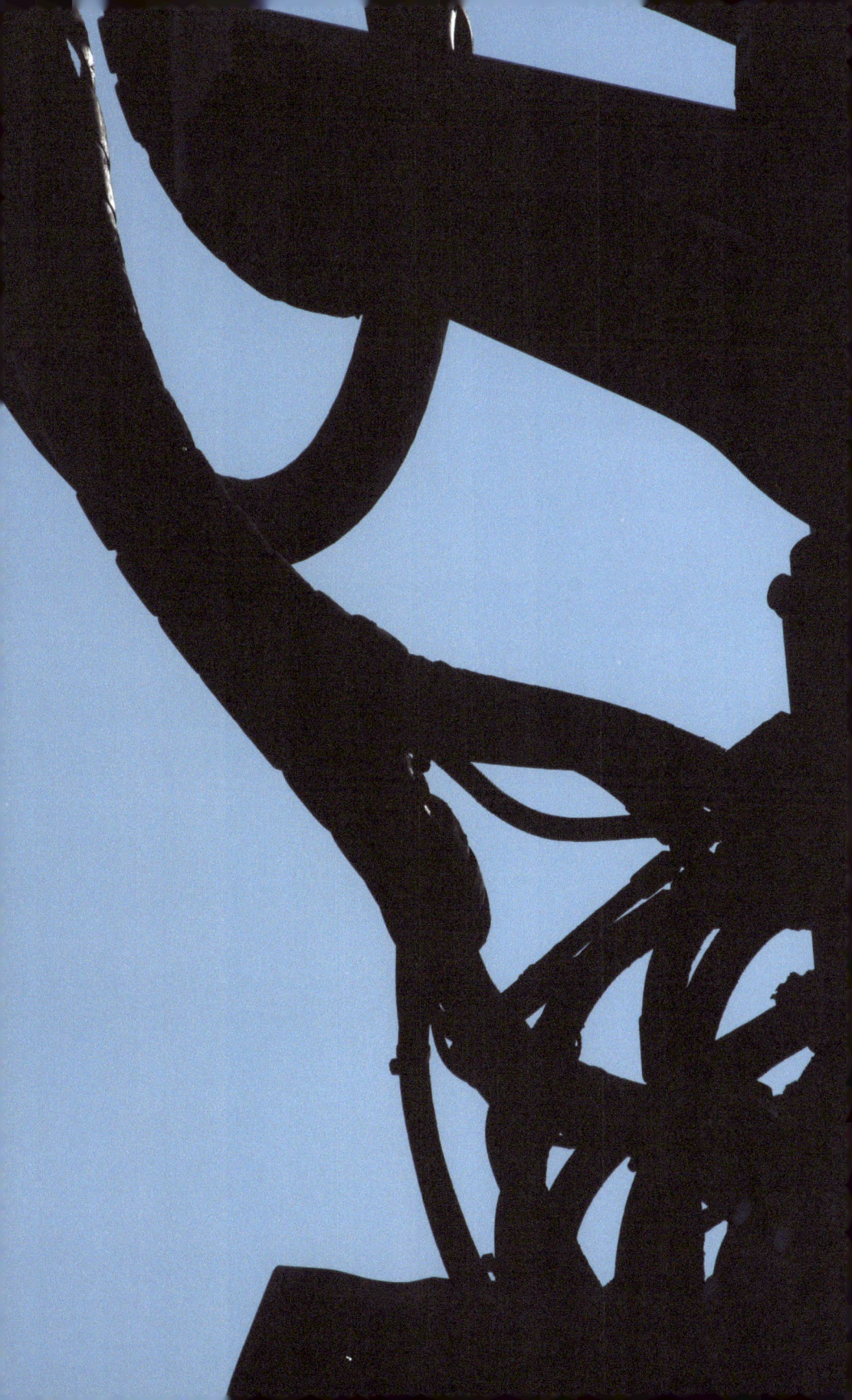

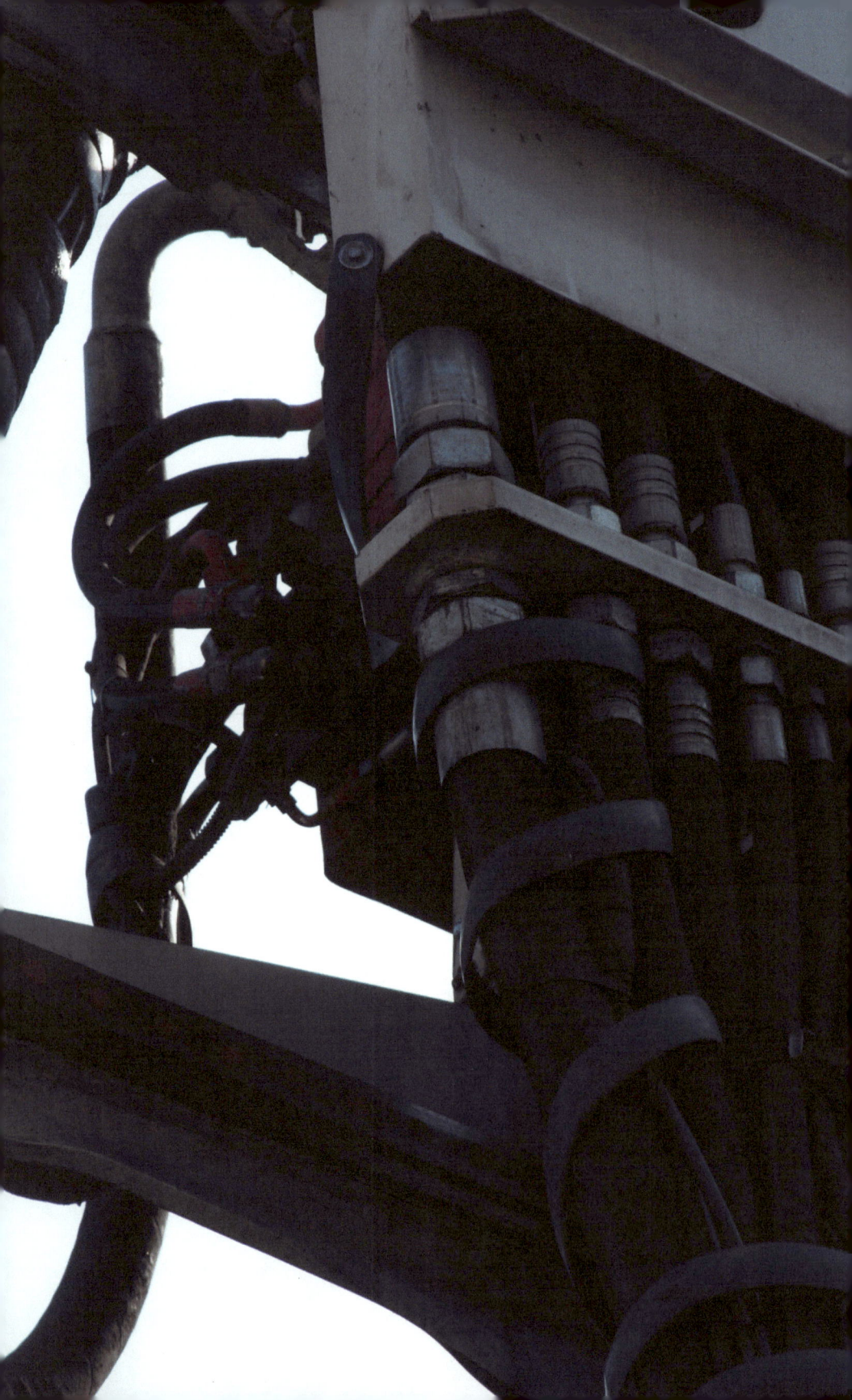

Han knew, based on his own exploding symptoms, that there was nothing the guards could do. Thousands would be dead within the quarter hour. Perhaps one in ten thousand would be alive by the end of the week.

The guards didn't know that, and perhaps it wouldn't have changed their actions even if they did. They all shot her at the same time, just as the doors of a small Tube opened at Han's left, letting off several dozen new passengers. In the front of the group, the person Han had least expected to ever see in person – President Eclark.

The President waved as the excited crowds began cheering. He smiled at his ruse of having taken the least expected route to the convention. Almost no one knew of the Whitehorse Mine's direct tube to Washington, so no would expect the President to arrive by way of Whitehorse and Duluth. People plotting trouble because of LuniGrab would have all their resources positioned around the Chicago Minnesota airport, which would be gridlocked for hours.

As Han's consciousness faded, he could see the President take a deep breath and wave joyfully again to the crowds. The President moved past Han toward the Duluth Tube. Right before blacking out, Han saw a slight flicker of puzzlement come to the President's face. The President momentarily touched his throat and coughed lightly.

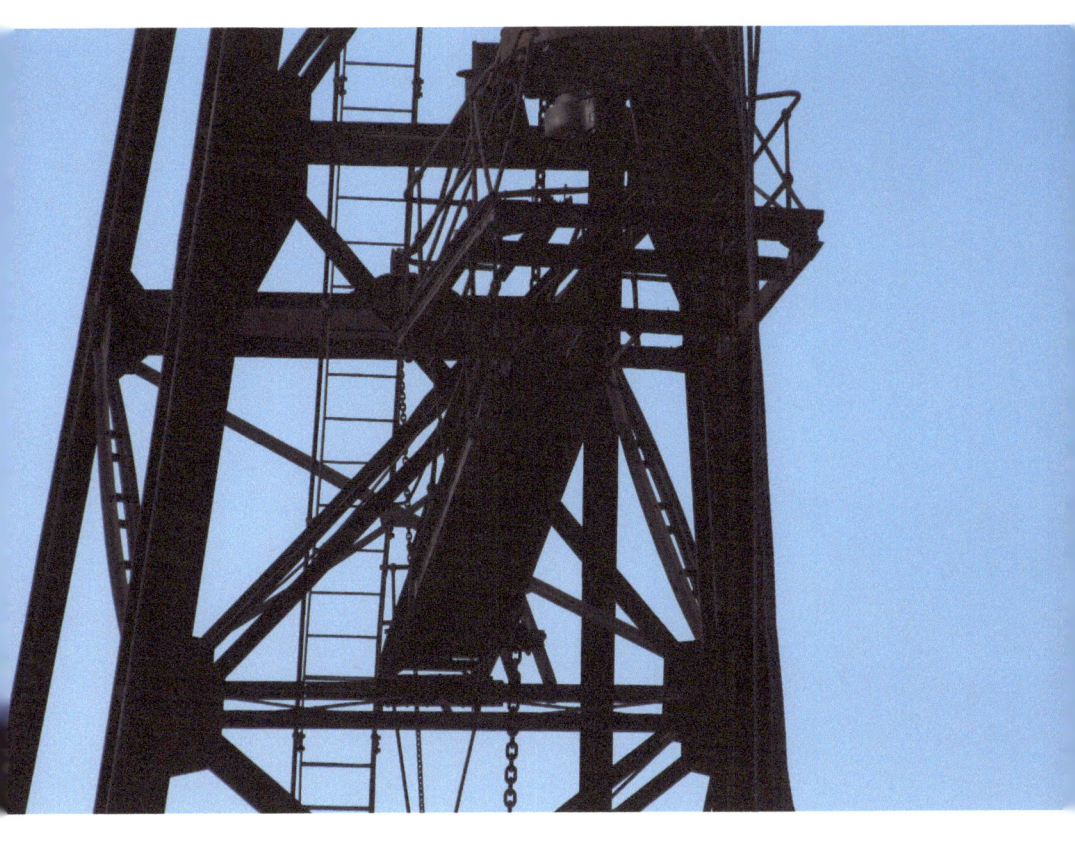

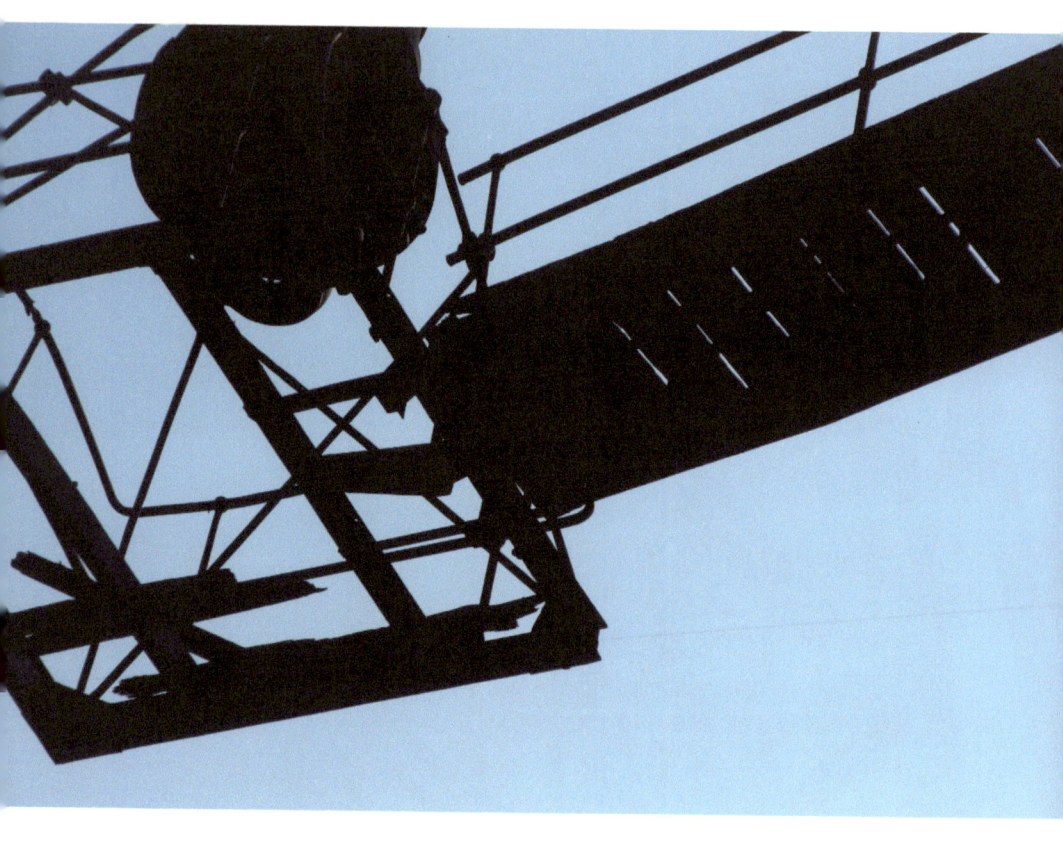

Then Han's vision went black. Han fell to the ground. Before his hearing faded away, Han heard coughing, lots of coughing, coughing all around him. A massive pain exploded in his chest and all his thoughts disappeared.

Emptiness.

A deep, deep void. A cottony cocoon around his senses.
Everything seemed to come from some distant galaxy.

He vaguely knew that someone was touching his arm, but his
arm seemed thousands of years and millions of miles away.
His consciousness was misty, his memories scattered and light,
wispy, in danger of disappearing altogether.

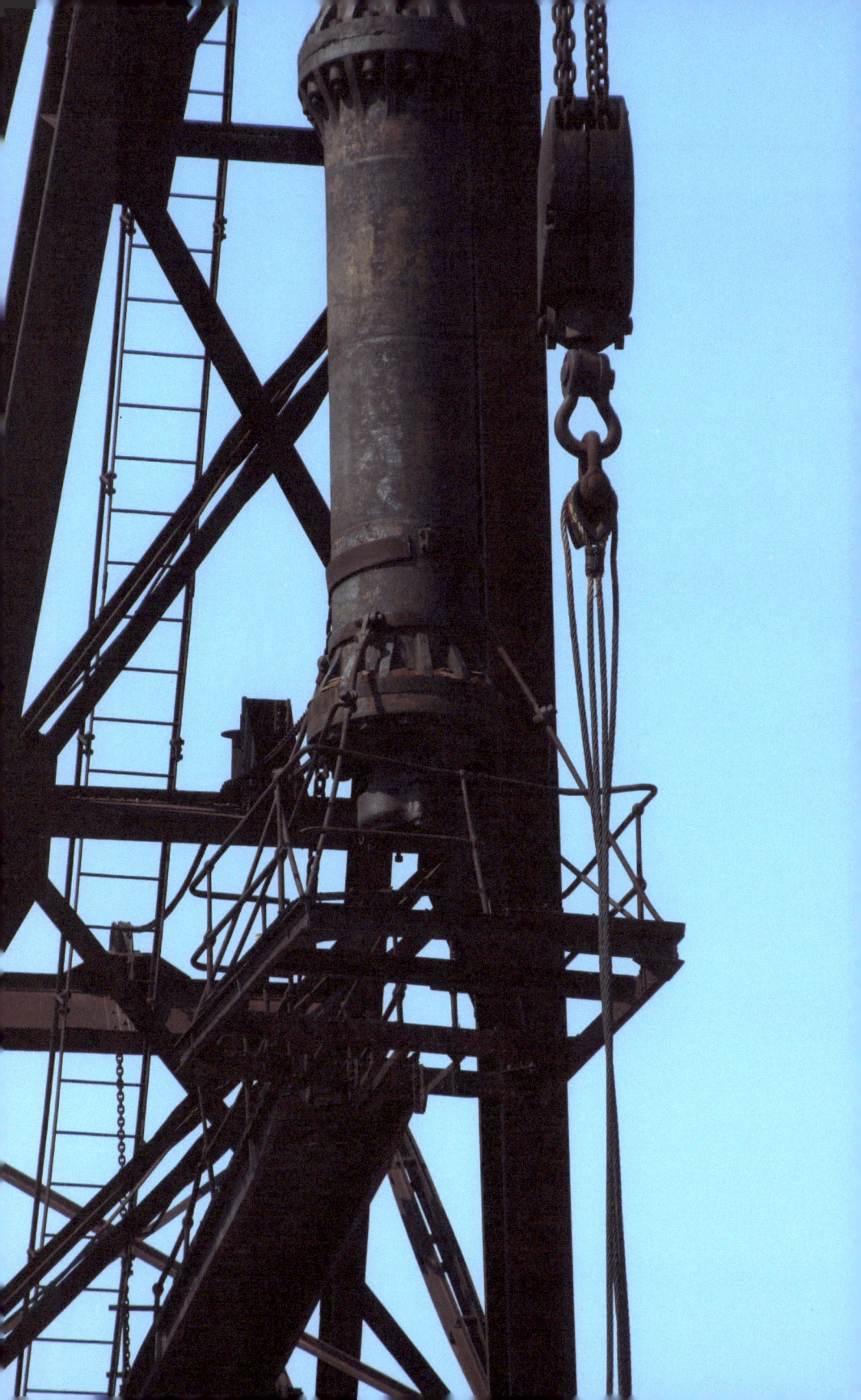

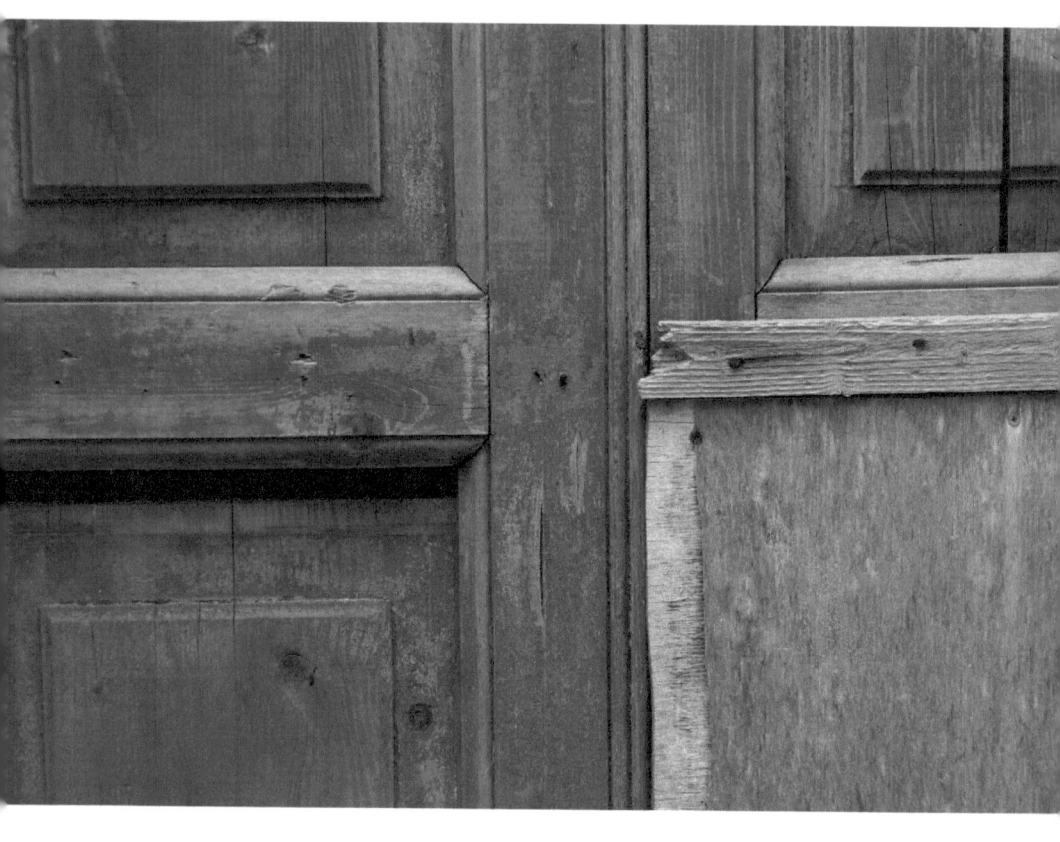

He felt a sting on his arm, then pain, overwhelming pain.

He could reconcile all the wispiness with what he'd guessed about death. But the sudden *pain*. How could he be cut off from everything and in so much *pain?*

His body was racked with it. Every cell, every fiber, every organ was experiencing multiple layers of pain: a dull pain, a hot pain, a stabbing pain, an intermittent pain, a constant pain. He wondered how there was room for it all in his brain. Maybe that was why his memories were so jumbled and faded.

He lost consciousness.

When he awoke, Han knew time had passed, but he could not say how long. Could the pain possibly be less?

The pain was so consuming, surely it wasn't less. How could it be less and be this intense?

If this was death and death was forever, Han was in a bad, bad spot.

Han was sweating. He drifted out again.

It was like that for what seemed like forever. It could have been just moments; he wasn't sure.

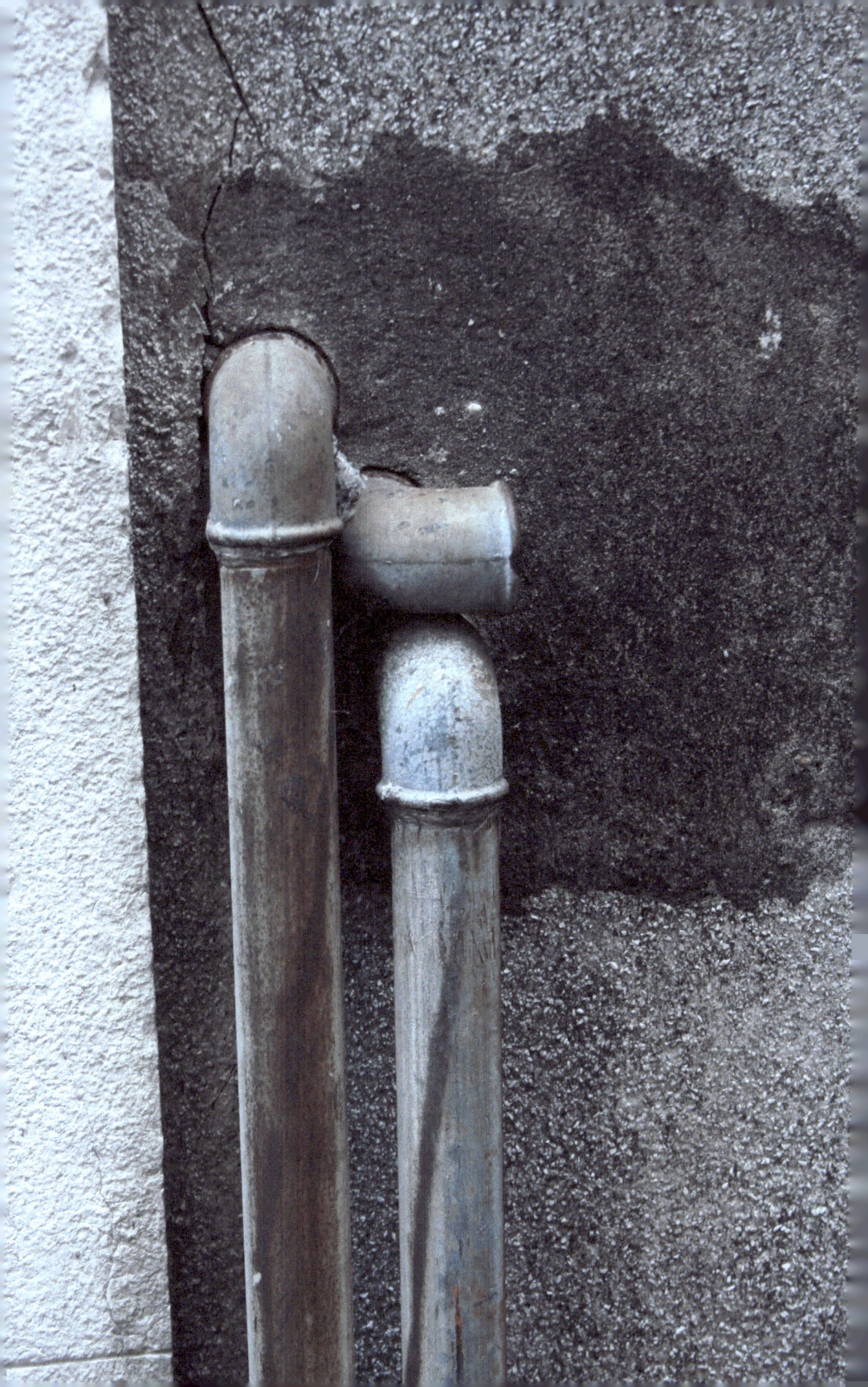

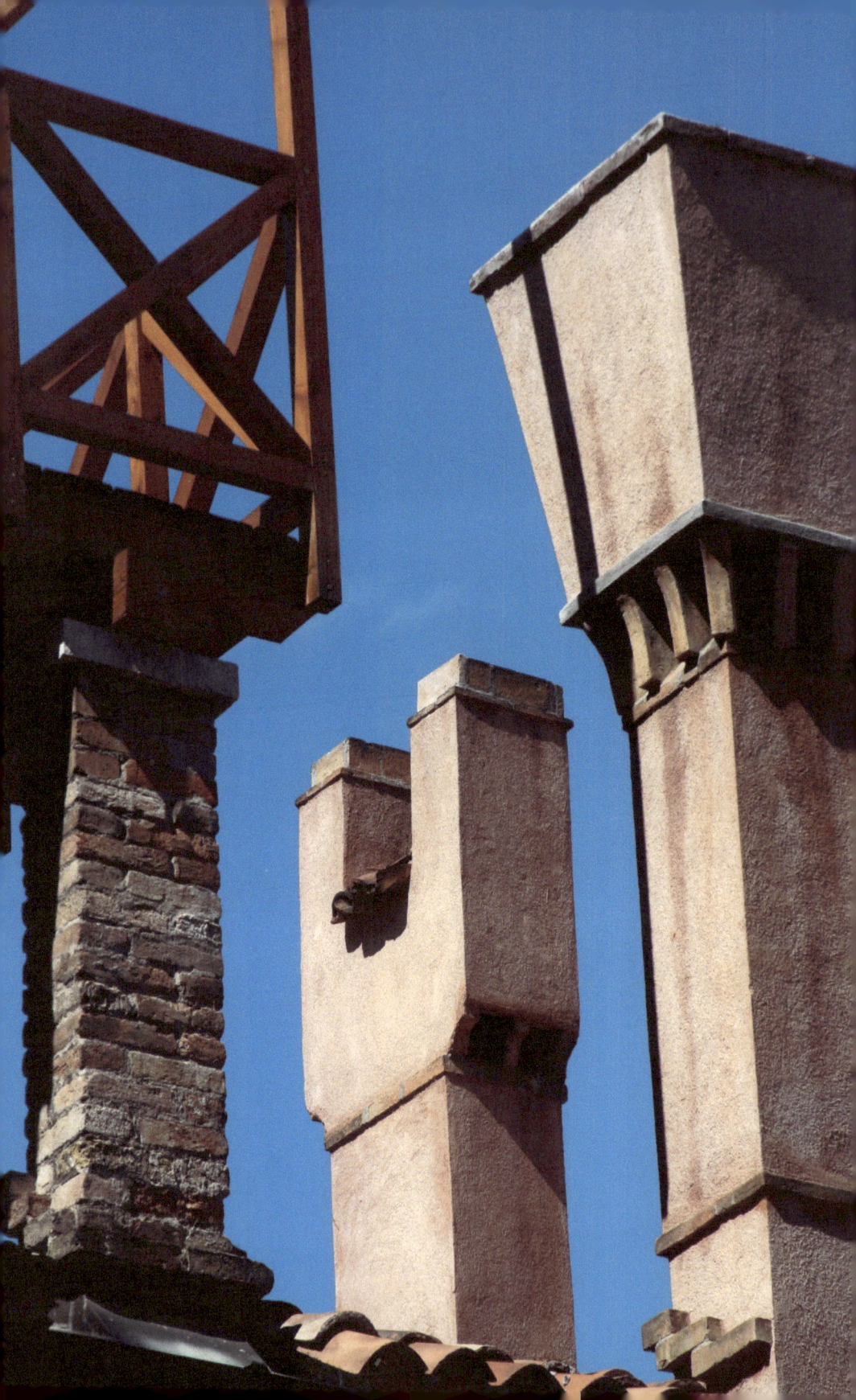

Then light. Piercing.

Thousands of miles away he heard a rumbling voice in slow motion.

"N o t   t o o   f a s t .

A   l i t t l e   l e s s .

L   e s s   .

G o   s l o w l y .

N o t   t o o   m u c h ."

Another explosion of pain, and everything disappeared.

~~

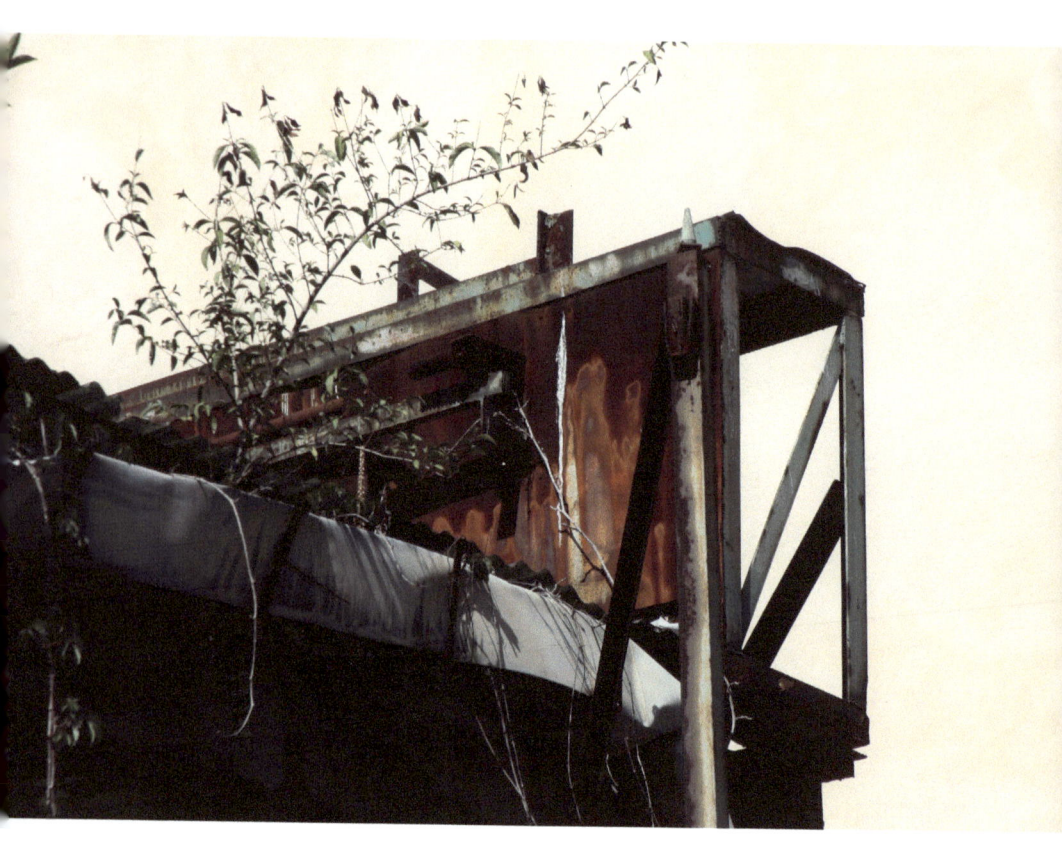

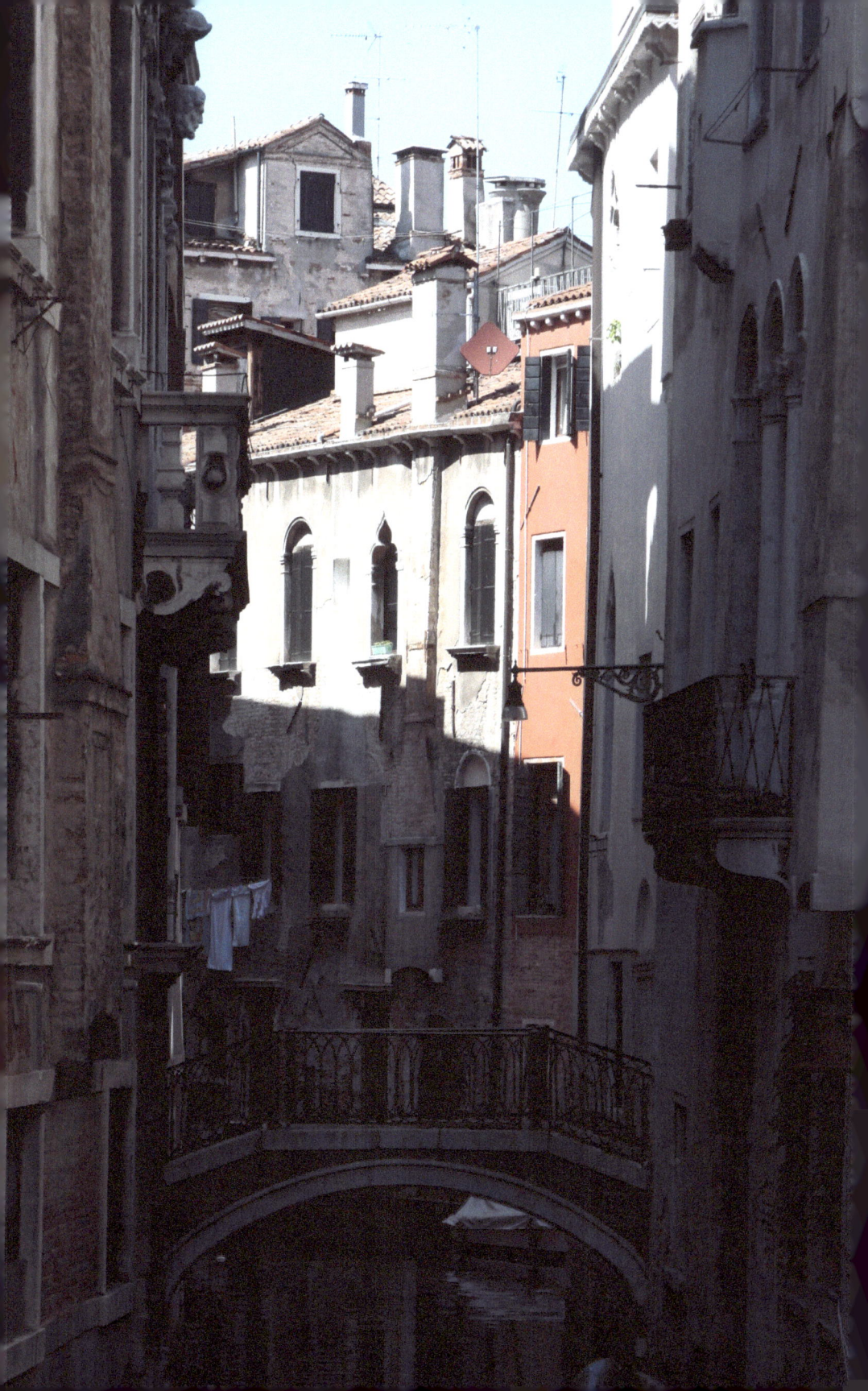

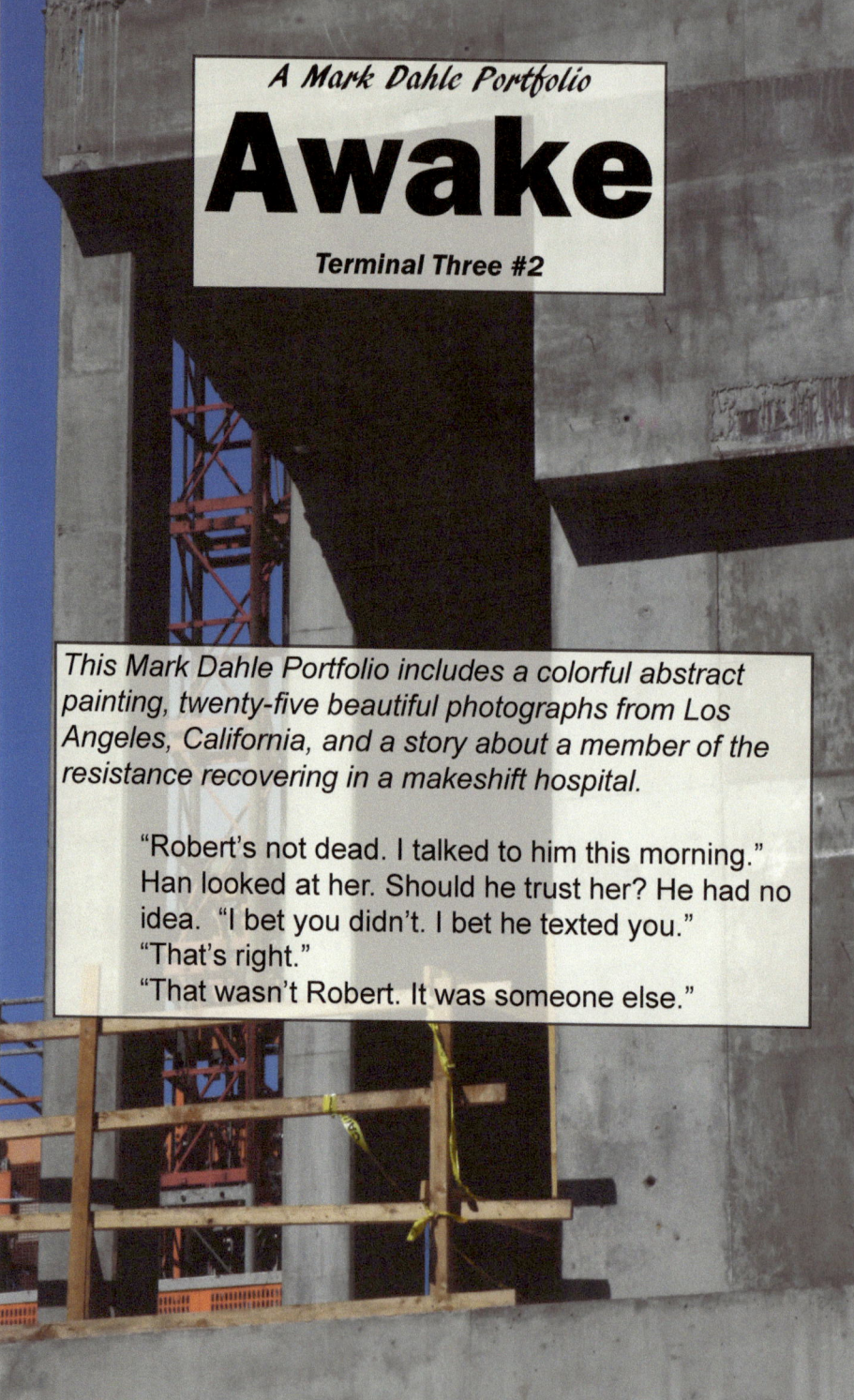

A Mark Dahle Portfolio

Awake

Terminal Three #2

This Mark Dahle Portfolio includes a colorful abstract painting, twenty-five beautiful photographs from Los Angeles, California, and a story about a member of the resistance recovering in a makeshift hospital.

"Robert's not dead. I talked to him this morning." Han looked at her. Should he trust her? He had no idea. "I bet you didn't. I bet he texted you." "That's right." "That wasn't Robert. It was someone else."

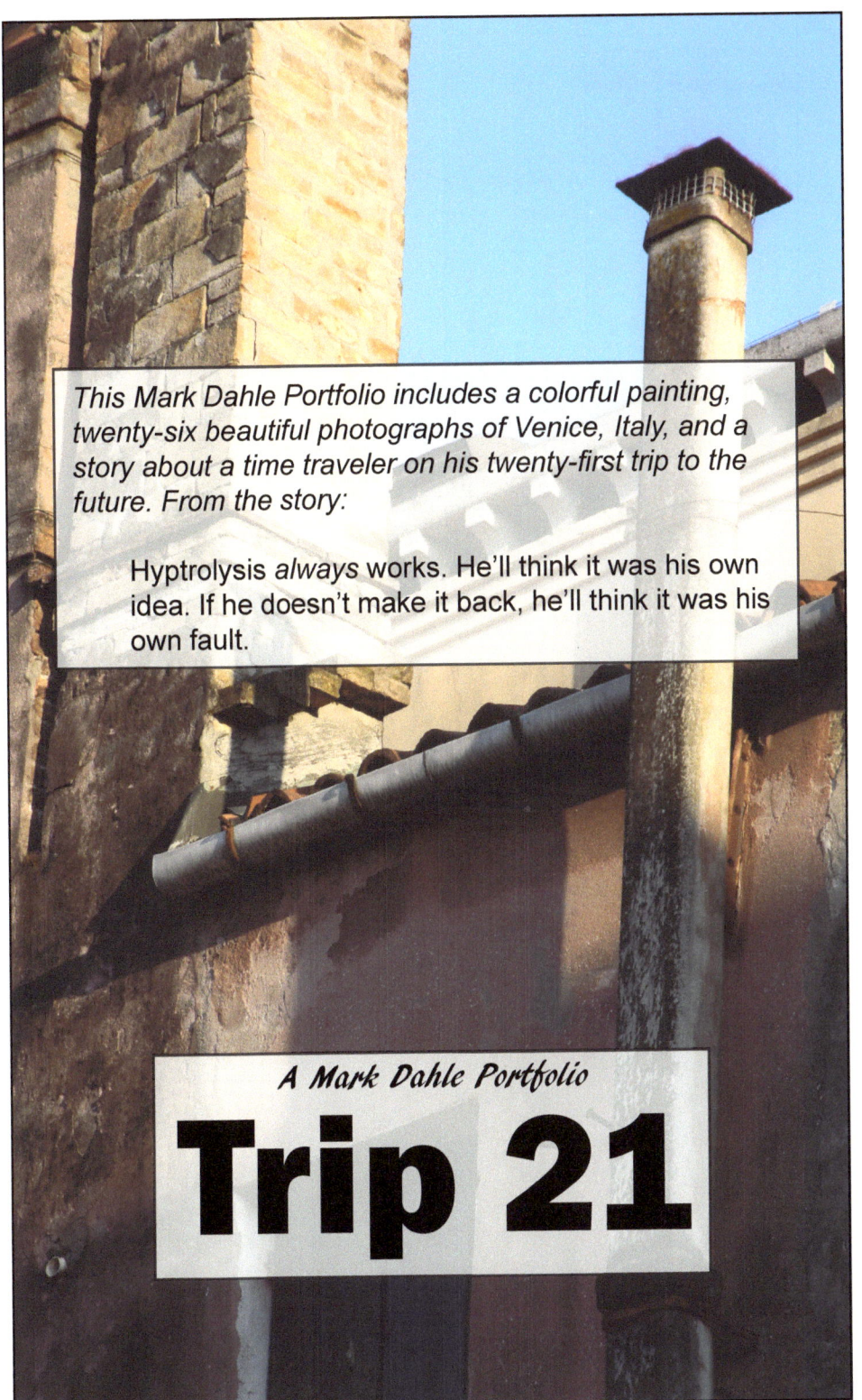

This Mark Dahle Portfolio includes a colorful painting, twenty-six beautiful photographs of Venice, Italy, and a story about a time traveler on his twenty-first trip to the future. From the story:

Hyptrolysis *always* works. He'll think it was his own idea. If he doesn't make it back, he'll think it was his own fault.

A Mark Dahle Portfolio

Trip 21

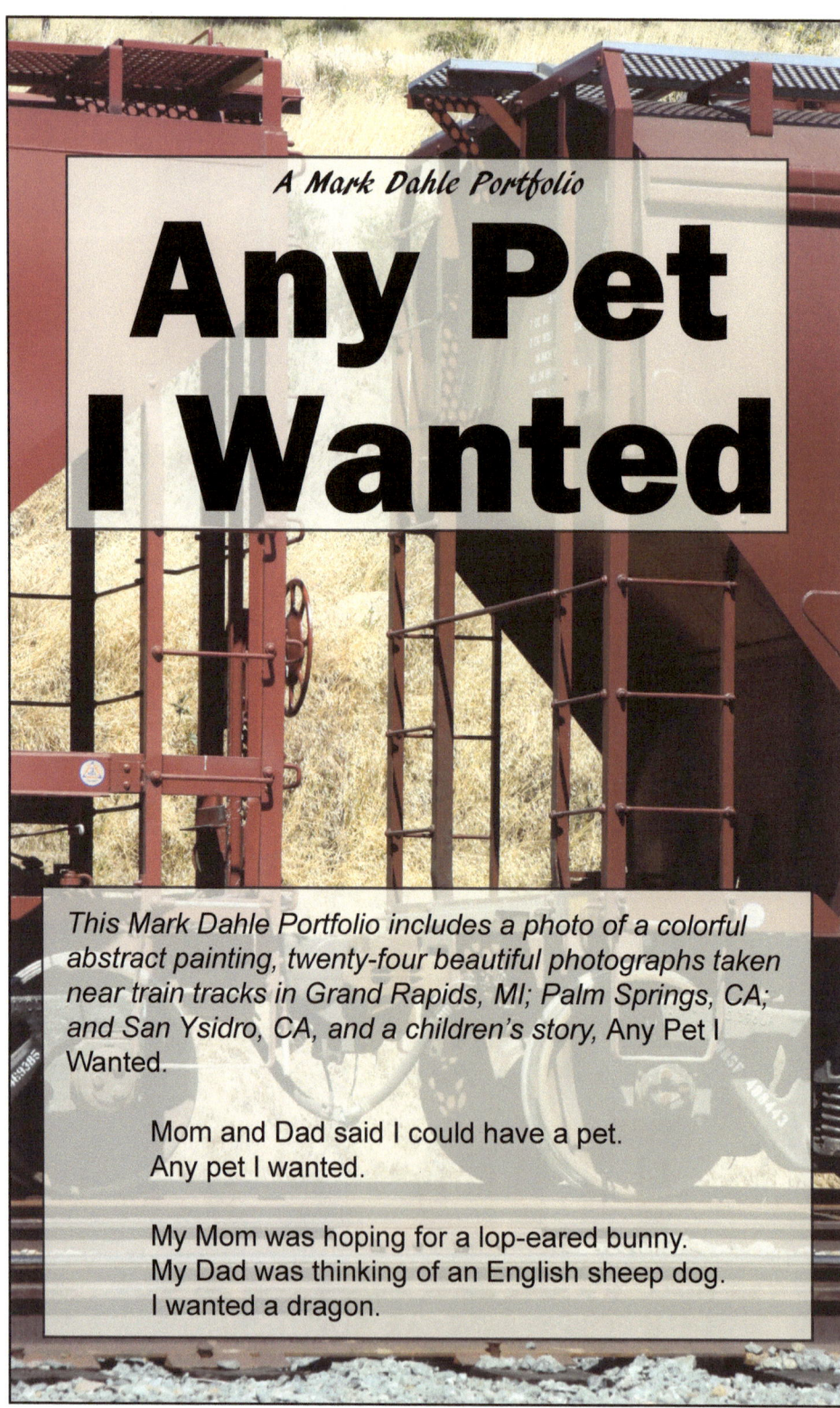

A Mark Dahle Portfolio

Any Pet I Wanted

This Mark Dahle Portfolio includes a photo of a colorful abstract painting, twenty-four beautiful photographs taken near train tracks in Grand Rapids, MI; Palm Springs, CA; and San Ysidro, CA, and a children's story, Any Pet I Wanted.

Mom and Dad said I could have a pet.
Any pet I wanted.

My Mom was hoping for a lop-eared bunny.
My Dad was thinking of an English sheep dog.
I wanted a dragon.

www.ingramcontent.com/pod-product-compliance
Lightning Source LLC
Chambersburg PA
CBHW040902180526
45159CB00001B/494